T0157636

FITLY FRAMED TOGETHER

The Bible

Mike Culpepper

WestBow Press books may be ordered through booksellers or by contacting:

WestBow Press
A Division of Thomas Nelson
1663 Liberty Drive
Bloomington, IN 47403
www.westbowpress.com
1-(866) 928-1240

ISBN: 978-1-4908-0527-6 (sc)
ISBN: 978-1-4908-0528-3 (hc)
ISBN: 978-1-4908-0529-0 (e)

Library of Congress Control Number: 2013914821

Printed in the United States of America.

WestBow Press rev. date: 9/11/2013

I am most grateful to God for my life and
the abilities He has given me.

I am thankful for my dear wife, Cindy, and I dedicate
this book to her because of her love and patience
for these past forty plus years of marriage.

Now therefore you are no more strangers and foreigners, but fellow citizens with the saints, and of the household of God; And are built upon the foundation of the apostles and prophets, Jesus Christ himself being the chief corner stone, In whom all the building fitly framed together grows unto a holy temple in the Lord, in whom you are built together for a habitation of God through the Spirit.

—Ephesians 2:19–22.

TABLE OF CONTENTS

LIST OF TABLES

PREFACE

People need to know about God … and man's relationship with Him. Eternity is a long time! Too often, people will act and talk as if they understand the nature of God, but in fact, they do not have a clue. People may even display a belief in God, yet in their convictions, they do not relate to Jesus or most any concepts of the Bible for that matter.

I recently sat next to a man on a lengthy airplane ride and carried on a conversation about God, Jesus, politics, etc. As he mentioned some things about God and Jesus and what he thought about going to heaven and living on the earth, it was apparent that he did not know much about biblical stories or anything about the Bible. I asked him if he had ever read the Bible, and he said no. He had never even seen a Bible, much less read from it. I then asked how he came up with the ideas and beliefs that he had without ever reading the Bible. His basic reply was this: "Well, that is just what everybody believes. Besides, the Bible should not be taken literally anyway. It is just a bunch of stuff that was written by a bunch of people with a lot of time on their hands."

I am reminded of a story of a man who had a talking parrot. Unfortunately, the language the parrot used was filthy and vulgar. On one occasion, following a crude and coarse verbal tantrum by the parrot, the man, who was furious, threw it into the freezer of his refrigerator. But after a while, he began to feel bad, and a short while later, he took the parrot out of the freezer. Cold and shivering, the parrot began to speak, but in a stoic, nonvulgar, and straightforward tone. "I sincerely regret the words and the language I have spoken, and I apologize for any harm and offense I may have caused you." The man was stunned. The parrot continued, "Oh, by the way, what offense did that other bird commit?" (He was referring to the frozen turkey he had seen in the freezer.)

Without considering the consequences, we act. But oftentimes in our lives, we say and do things because we are not aware or do not fully understand what we are doing and why. However, if we can better understand our situations through education and proper learning through proper sources, we will be much better off. The problem with reading and understanding the greatest source of education and wisdom, the Bible, is that there is much misunderstanding at the outset. Even those who may attend a Sunday school class or go to Bible studies may have difficulty in comprehending the scope and breadth of the Bible.

There are many commentaries and study helpers made for the Bible. It has been described that even if all the oceans were made of ink instead of saltwater, it still would not be enough ink to expound upon the Scriptures. In my years of studying and teaching, I have learned a great deal. Thirty years ago, my young adult Sunday school class gave me a Bible. Since then, as I have prepared for Sunday school lessons, listened to sermons, and attended seminars and conferences, I have marked, underlined, scribbled notes, and otherwise written observations and statements of biblical study in the margins and pages of that Bible. Using the knowledge, background, and my reflections on Scripture, I desire to best condense and comment on the Bible. In this undertaking, I have researched Scripture and have carefully examined Old and New Testament passages alike. Of course, the belief is that if it is indeed the Word of God, what it says is meaningful and very important. Most people, however, do not have that belief; many even claim that the Bible is a hoax.

It is the intent of this writing to illustrate that the Bible was put together in such a way as to claim that it is the Word of God, not necessarily because of *what* it says (although this certainly is critical) but *how* it was put together. In this text, I have utilized the King James Version, trying to centralize on the most accurate and popular version of the Bible.

If people can be better convinced that the Bible is indeed the true, real Word of God, they may well adopt it to a greater extent, take it more seriously, and study it more. As architects, engineers, and construction workers design, build, and put together bridges and buildings—and these structures stand firm—so it is with the Bible. It is literally designed and put together word by word—and it stands firm. The Bible has the framework and fabric showing that it is indeed fitly framed together.

Mike Culpepper

Mike Culpepper
Author

INTRODUCTION

The worldwide sales of the Bible have consistently been at the top or near the top for more than a century. It certainly remains the foremost printed material of all time and remains the most notable feature in the life of all mankind. So begins the journey of *Fitly Framed Together.* All or parts of the Bible have been translated into more than two thousand different languages, certainly more than any other book.

The way the Bible was originally written and eventually published in modern times and the way it has endured the logistics of nature and the tainted existence of mankind is a story in and of itself. Although the Bible is a book that may be published and purchased, many do not fathom or understand its content. Countless people have never read it in the first place. There has always been a never-ending plethora of questions and various "interpretations" of the Scriptures. Secular adults may not think of the Bible as the "Word of God". They certainly do not view the Bible as a guide for their life. On the other hand, although "Christians" may claim to believe the Bible is God's Word, they may live their whole life with little understanding of the purpose and nature of the Bible.

Someone has said that the word *Bible* is an acronym for "Basic Instruction Before Leaving Earth." It is certainly a book containing instructions, but it is not just a book of rules and regulations. Though it represents the testament of the Word of God, many never are able to experience the nature of the one true God because they never experience His true Word. Like many other things in life, many people seem to get off on good things but miss out on the best thing—fellowship with an almighty yet loving God and enjoying everlasting life!

For many, the Bible is seen as a mysterious, difficult book. However, the Bible says, "I have not spoken in secret, in a dark place on the earth" (Isaiah 45:19). It also reads, "Your Word is a lamp unto my pathway, a light unto my feet" (Psalm 119:105), and "For the Lord is a God of knowledge" (1 Samuel 2:3). Consequently, although it may seem to be difficult reading, the truth is that God, in His desire for us to understand Him more and more, has indeed penned a text worthy of reading and understanding.

The difficulty of understanding its content lies in the fact that it comes from an infinite God to a finite man. The Bible's words come from an unlimited, omnipotent God and are supposed to be understood by a limited and sinful man. There are certainly those who look upon the Bible like they do the literary texts of Socrates, Plato, or any other worldly human writing that come from the same limited boundary of mankind as does the interpretations of them.

In fact, there are those who have called the Bible a hoax and thus claim that it is not what it has been touted to be throughout the centuries. But the purpose of this text is not to act as a Bible commentary, refute the naysayers, or debate Scripture. The focus is to profile the Bible as fitly framed together and to let the reader be the judge.

So what makes the Bible different? What is it about the Bible that lends it as the authentic Word of God—the *real* Scripture? In order for man to scrutinize the Bible as the ultimate authority of God, all one has to do is study it. The Bible is indeed organized in a way that no other literary work can boast. The contents of any literature can always be scrutinized and interpreted. However, one of the intriguing aspects of the Bible is not only its content but also how it is (was) put together.

No other literary text has had a greater effect on mankind. No other writing has described the history and defined theology as the Bible. No other writing has the background and etiology. No other manuscript or publication has endured the tribulations of history as the Bible. From cover to cover, from Genesis to Revelation, no other book has been fitly framed together.

At the outset, the Bible was written by approximately forty different writers over a period of fifteen hundred years. These writers included fishermen, kings, farmers, teachers, physicians, public officials, and others whose interests ranged from poetry, drama, science, history, and law, among a few. Yet these attributes of people and lifestyles harmoniously became united. No other book or reference can claim such. The Bible is truly fitly framed together!

Some of these authors may or may not have been gifted, but they all were enabled by God, not simply inspired to write. Thus, it is fair to say that the Bible is not just the inspired writings of humans. Nowhere does the Bible say that its authors were inspired. Truly, there have been many inspired writings (and songs) by man, but the Bible is not one of them. The Bible was "authored" by the Holy Spirit. "For the prophecy came not in old time by the will of man: but holy men of God spake as they were directed by the Holy Ghost" (2 Peter 1:21). In other words, the Bible was not written by inspired men. As such, the Bible does not contain the Word of God. It *is* the Word of God! Of course, man had to be the instrument used to write the Bible because God made man! What other earthly creation could literally pen the revelation of God?

In fact, it is the Bible or the Word of God that inspires. There is the story of the music of Handel and his musical work, "The Messiah." But how did it come about? Who wrote the words? Handel did not. Charles Jennings was a wealthy man who liked to write poetry. He had written some poetry, and Handel had written some tunes; however, they were all flops. Then on one occasion, Jennings wrote the words to "The Messiah," of course taken from the scripture. Handel was at first unwilling to write any music to the words. He could not afford another flop. But when he read the words, he was moved to write the music, which he completed in only twenty-three days.

The first performance was at a fund-raising event that King George II attended. At the time, many "preachers/ministers" were against using a musical of God for fund-raising. But at its initial performance,

King George was so moved that he stood at the "Hallelujah Chorus." This was more than 250 years ago. God's Word "inspired" Jennings, which inspired Handel, which inspired King George. Ever since that first performance, it has been "tradition" to stand at the singing of the "Hallelujah Chorus." Throughout time, the Word of God has continued to inspire others.

Therefore, since it is God's literal writings (and not that of some inspired man), it resulted in the infallible Word of the God who created all things. It is free from error and thus is absolutely trustworthy and authoritative. "For the Word of God is living and powerful, and sharper than any two edged sword, piercing even to the dividing asunder of soul and spirit, and of the joints and marrow, and is a discerner of thoughts and intents of the heart" (Hebrews 4:12). "All scripture is given by inspiration of God, and is profitable for doctrine, for reproof, for instruction in righteousness: that the man of God may be perfect thoroughly unto all good works" (2 Timothy 3:16–17). In this reference, the word "inspiration" was coined by Paul from the Greek word theopneustos". "Theo" has the meaning of God (theology) and we get pneumo or pneumonia (air breathed...lungs) from pneustos. Thus the Bible is literally "God-Breathed". Men were not just "inspired" enough to write, but that the words of God were "God-breathed" and man was the instrument for these words. If one is to view the Bible as God's word, it must have these characteristics. Otherwise, the Bible can only be seen as another of man's doings, not that of God, and thus not held in highest esteem.

Unlike other "writings," the Bible is not a just a book of prophecies, warnings, human stories, and philosophical sayings ascribing rules and regulations of life. It is a book of life. There is a central truth, a same line of thought and portrayal of concepts. Not only was the Bible penned by separate individuals, but the time frame in which it was written covered more than 1,500 years. No other literary work can make that claim. In addition, as it is studied, it portrays the infinite to the finite, characterizing the spirit to the flesh, defining the unlimited to the limited, and it does so in an infallible, errorless fashion! This truly must be a fitly framed together text.

The Bible says, "For my thoughts are not your thoughts neither are your ways my ways, said the Lord" (Isaiah 55:8), and most often, there is confusion and misunderstanding. There is a story in the tenth chapter of John in which Jesus is using Scripture to reason with the Jews. Jesus was trying to explain that He and the Father were one (God).

> The Jews answered him saying, For a good work we stone you not, but for blasphemy; and because that you, being a man makes yourself God. Jesus answered them, Is it not written in your law, I said you are gods? If he called them gods, unto whom the word of God came, and the scripture is true forever; Say of him, whom the father hath sanctified, and sent into the world, You blaspheme; because I said I am the Son of God? (John 10:33–6)

Jesus quoted Psalms 82:6, "I have said you are gods; and all of you are children of the Most High." Therefore, even Jesus was referring to Scripture (or the known Bible at that time). And the Scripture He was referencing was written hundreds and hundreds of years ago. If Jesus referenced the Scripture, there must be some continuity of Scripture of past and present, at least up to the time of Christ. And if there is that need of reference and there is continuity of Scripture and if it was utilized by Jesus, then further investigation of the Bible as being fitly framed together there must at least be some effort of exploration regarding the Bible.

Issues certainly arises from those who may read "some" or "parts" of the Bible and do not "connect the dots" in trying to understand what God is actually trying to reveal through His Word. Numerous times, Jesus said to those who were to supposed to already know Scripture, "You do err, not knowing scriptures nor the power of God" (Matthew 22:29).

The Bible was written for application in one's life, not necessarily for interpretation to simply be discussed. To be sure, understanding language for communication and direction is critical. But when one has a lifestyle (already) and seeks to "interpret" Scripture for their "agenda," then in reality, the Bible will not be of any true benefit.

It has been revealed that in America, 76 percent profess to be Christians, yet only 70 percent believe in hell, 20 percent attend a church service in any week, almost one fourth (24 percent) of professing Christians never read the Bible. Only 5 percent tithe and less than 10 percent attend a church twelve times a year or more. Only 28 percent of Americans believe the Bible is the actual word of God and 64 percent of American adults believe that Jesus rose from the dead.[1,2,3]. Certainly, these numbers do not add up. We have even had governmental elected officials who proclaim to be Christian but also say that "there are other ways to get into heaven." Jesus emphatically stated, "I am the way, the truth, and the life. No one comes to the Father but by me" (John 14:6).

To be sure, there have been numerous books written that have been proclaimed to be from God. There are some religions that claim that their "god" is the same God of the Bible. But these claims, of course, cannot be true. If the Bible, which was written by the God of the Bible, is not used in their faith, then the god of which they speak cannot be the God of the Bible because the descriptions and accounts do not come from the Bible. In other words, because the descriptions and accounts of a god are chief and primary to one's religious beliefs, the source of these "accounts and descriptions" is paramount!

In the Bible, there are the accounts and descriptions and doctrines of Scripture, which surpass the comprehension of man, lending credence that Scripture was indeed written by God and not just inspired man. Yet the Bible is fully understandable, and it is the duty of a believer to study the Bible and learn and grow. "Study to show yourself approved unto God, a workman that needs not to be ashamed, rightly dividing the word of truth" (2 Timothy 2:15).

Thus, considering the logistics of how and when the Bible was written, the oneness or unity of the Bible is a miracle itself. Unlike other religious books written by one author, the Bible itself is actually a collection of books and references. The word "Bible" has its origin from the word Byblos, which was the name of an ancient Phoenician city. A major export of the city was papyrus, on which ancient text were written. Thus, there were *byblos* books. The Greeks eventually incorporated the word *biblia* in its vocabulary, from which we get the word "bibliography." The Bible is indeed a collection of references from about forty authors and penned over a 1,500-year span. Thus, it is amazing that this book called the Bible ever came together in the first place, much less survived.

If the Bible is true, describing the very nature of God (and in its discourse reveals a true Satan), then Satan would no less wage war against such writings. A notable plan by Satan then, would be to attempt to remove the Scripture altogether. Indeed, it would seem that Scripture would have eventually ceased to exist with the passing of so much time. And this would be the case if Scripture were of man. But since Scripture is of God, it has survived. Therefore, any discourse on the fabric of Scripture must begin with its author and protector—God! No other book or writing has endured the blight of humanity, ironically the very nature for which it was written.

Jesus said in Matthew 24:35, "Heaven and earth will pass away, but my word will remain forever." Peter wrote, "Having been born again, not of corruptible seed but incorruptible, through the word of God which lives and abides forever, because all flesh is as grass and all the glory of m an as the flowers of the grass. The grass withers and its flowers fall away, but the word of the Lord endures forever" (1 Peter 1:23–5).

Unlike other texts, history has shown that persons and circumstances have indeed attempted to stamp out the Bible. In 168 BC, the Seleucid monarch Antiochus IV had the Jewish "Book of the Law" torn and burned. In 303, the Roman Emperor Diocletian decreed to kill all Christians and extinguish the Bible. In 1242, the French king Louis IX ordered the burning of twelve thousand copies of the Talmud in Paris. Public burnings of the Talmud were also done in 1553 and 1568. No other book or collection of writings has been subject to such defamation and persecution.

Even the Catholic Church tried to deny the Bible in the language of the common people by persecuting the likes of John Wycliff, William Tyndale, Martin Luther, and others who had developed translated Scripture for "common" people to read. In 1773, the French writer and philosopher Voltaire boasted that within a hundred years, the only Bibles that would be in existence would be those for antiquarian curiosity[4,5]. It is said that the Geneva Bible Society purchased his home and now uses it as a bookstore to exclusively sell Bibles!

Thomas Paine said, "Fifty years after I die, the Bible will be obsolete.[5]" In 1939, as part of an "expunging effort" to rid Nazi Germany of books not in keeping with the philosophy of German life, the Nazi leader Hitler burned copies of the Bibles. However, in spite of these attempts to rid and purge the world of the Bible, the Bible still exists. Truly, no other book or literature writings have existed and have passed through the ages of time.

The Bible begins with the following: "In the beginning God created—" (Genesis 1:1). The Bible closes with this passage: I am the Alpha and Omega, the beginning and the end, the first and the last" (Revelation 22:13). Everything in between is equally important!

Therefore, this writing is an attempt to "tie" together the threads that hold the Old and New Testaments together. The Bible is a tapestry, woven of God's great nature. There certainly are many threads creating this tapestry. It is interesting that Paul was a tent maker. He could certainly pen fitly framed together. In his letters of the New Testament, he tied together and wove many of the things in the Old Testament, such as the temple, the priests, the sacrifices, and blood, with New Testament things, such as Christ and the church. It was he who coined the phrase "fitly framed together" (Ephesians 2:21). So what makes the Bible so different? What makes the text of the Bible so different from other religious writings? What makes it so fitly framed together? This text is not intended to be another "documentary" but an understanding of the true meaning of the Bible and the fabric that holds it together.

To be sure, the Bible is God's Word to us. Many times the Bible says, "I am the Lord your God." It is not a book written by someone who says that there is a god. God Himself says it! "The Lord Almighty has sworn, surely, as I have planned, so shall it will be, and as I have purposed, so it will stand" (Isaiah 14:24). "But the plans of the Lord stand firm forever, the purposes of his heart through all generations" (Psalm 33:11). And consider this passage: "Many, O Lord my God are the wonders you have done. The things you have planned for us no one can recount to you; were I to speak and tell of them, they would be too many to declare" (Psalm 40:5).

Thus, there was "a beginning" (created by God), and there will be an "ending" of time (as determined by God). The Bible, therefore, has "God's story" to us, and it is that He created, thus establishing existence. He created us and thus established reasons for our existence. He is not a god inflicting wrath upon a creation, but He is God who loves His creation and is committed to it.

Many words, books, and passages have been written that have moral overtones and that use personal, physical examples. *Aesop's Fables*, for example, contain stories that show by example the way we should live. However, because the Bible is more than just stories or examples, it is deeper in content. No other book, philosophical literature, or spiritual writing has done this, and they cannot be studied to the same extent as the Bible. Truly, no amount of ink and no volume of paper could begin to expound upon the nature of God's Word, although countless documentaries and representations will continue to be written.

The Bible is God's communication with man that attests as to why the physical and spiritual realms exist, not to mention how sin, death, and salvation came about, using iconic examples of mankind's everyday life. A major theme of the Bible is that there is but one and only one God. God has various attributes (i.e., the Father, Son, and Holy Spirit). For example, what am I, and what is my "purpose" in the world? I am a son to my father, a husband to my wife, a father to my children, a brother to my sisters, and so on. In each depiction, I have a special meaning and a special purpose.

God the Father is the planner, the Creator. Because sin and death are present, God the Son is the Father revealed as our Savior, saving us from our sins and giving us life. God the Holy Spirit is God the applier, applying His purpose in our lives as we live on this earth. We can see the purpose of the books of the Old Testament and the New Testament. And as we look at these characteristics of God, we will find Jesus throughout the books of the Bible.

Of course, a theme of the Bible is the idea of sin—what it is and the judgment for sin. But following the concept of sin is the realization of judgment for it and the redemption or payment for it, which includes the "Plan of Salvation." This is the purpose and need for Jesus. As such, this may be the biggest difference between the Bible and other religious texts. There are certainly other religions that believe in the existence of "God." But the Bible is explicit in its introduction and purpose of Jesus. Thus, the continuity and "oneness" of Scripture with respect to Jesus is a major focal point of the fact that the Bible is fitly framed together.

Oftentimes, as we examine and study very specific and poignant parts of the Bible, we can miss the "whole story." There are subtitles of the Bible that we sometimes overlook in order to see the whole picture. It would be similar to a thousand-piece puzzle. Each piece has a similar shape and color, but each is certainly distinct from one another. And each can be examined and scrutinized. But when they are all put together as one, then a beautiful picture can be seen. Oftentimes these picture puzzles are mounted and framed for viewing. However, if only one piece is missing, then the entire picture is "ruined," and the picture puzzle cannot be displayed. So it is with the Bible. There are indeed many "pieces" that must be put together in order for it all "to make sense." But if any one piece is missing, then none of the Bible can make complete sense. Therefore, the Bible, by its own nature, must be fitly framed together.

It is interesting how the descriptions and accounts of this magnitude are in harmony and in one accord. It is also interesting how the books of the Bible came together in later days and more recently in the different languages of mankind. These translations into so many languages were completed so that all peoples of the world could read and study Scripture. And for sure, no other book has been translated into so many languages. But the purpose and intent of biblical study is important. Should the Bible be scrutinized from a secular perspective, or are we supposed to take its message like food to strengthen and nourish our spiritual beings?

There is a story about Socrates, the Greek philosopher. Of course, Greek culture emphasized knowledge and education. There was a man who desired to sit at the feet of Socrates and soak in knowledge and learn from the famous Greek philosopher. He approached Socrates and inquired to learn from him. Without saying a word, Socrates led him to the ocean. They walked out onto the beach and into the water. The man thought this was strange. They walked out deeper and deeper into the water. Socrates still had not said one word. The man's curiosity began to run rampant. When they were neck-deep in the water, Socrates suddenly pushed the man's head under the water. The man was perplexed. After a few moments, the man began to gasp for air, but Socrates held him firmly under the water. The man began to fear for his life because he desperately needed air. At the last moment, Socrates released the man's head and let him up to breath. Surprised and bewildered, the man started panting and then asked, "Why did you do that?"

Socrates replied, "When you desire education like you desired the air you needed to breath, then will I teach you."

What one believes determines what one thinks. As one ponders the context, nature, and authority of the Bible, one's view of the Bible is critical. What one thinks determines what one does. And what one does determines his or her life ... now and forever. If we are to review and study the Bible, establishing the proper motivation to do so is important. Is the Bible "a" word, or is it "the" Word of God? Although many may consider the Bible to be "about God," Jesus is the cornerstone. Without Jesus, the Bible makes no sense. Without His death and resurrection, it makes no difference. Thus, the Bible must be fitly framed together.

REFERENCES

1. Rasmussen national poll. http//allchristiannews/poll-nearly 23-of American-believe-that-jesus/rose-from-the-dead (retrieved April 30, 2013)

2. Frank Newport, Gallop Poll (2006) www.gallop.com (retrieved April 30, 2013)

3. Greg Harrison, Few Churchgoes Tithe, Study Says. (2008) usatoday.com/news/religion/2008-5-31-tithing-church_N.htm. (retrieved April 30, 2013)

[Note. Many internet sites quote statistics of all types collected by polling services, including Barna Group, Gallop, Rasmussen and USA today.]

4. Why Do We Believe the Bible Is the Word Of God? The Fourth Reason. http://www.arabicbible.com/formuslims/questionsanswers/1555-why-we-believe-the-bible-is-the-word-of-god.html?start-4. (retrieved April 30, 2013

5. The Bible-Quotes From Famous Men. http:/www.why-the-bible-com/bible.htm. (retrieved April 30, 2013).

[Note. There are many internet sites that cite quotations from others. And some of these quotes are questioned by current groups for various reasons and intents.]

CHAPTER 1

Themes of the Bible

The Significance of What the Bible Is About

Many believe that it is the nature of many people to believe in supernatural events, but they fail to believe the Bible, which is full of supernatural events. There are no other texts in mankind that mention and describe as many supernatural events as the Bible.

However, the Bible still remains, as believed by Christians, the undisputed, infallible Word of God. It details God's true nature. It is the Bible (no other text) that has been written to attest to not just a god but the God. The fact is that all, literally *all* of God's Word fits together. From Genesis to Revelation, all of what has been written has one major theme, specifically the nature of God. It is revealed through the cross and Jesus Christ. One could say that unless you know the God of the Old Testament, you will never know the Christ of the New Testament. In other words, the Old Testament is the New Testament concealed. The New Testament is the Old Testament revealed. All of the Scripture must be considered.

A testament is a witnessed account, a description. The nature or characteristic of God is accurately described in these two testaments. Therefore, God had to write both the Old Testament and the New Testaments.

Of course, it is Satan's strategy to question Scripture and doubt its authenticity. As he tempted Eve in the Garden of Eden, Eve told the serpent that God had said that if they ate of the fruit of the knowledge of good and evil, they would die. But Satan said, "Surely you will not die" (Genesis 3:4), questioning the Word of God. In addition, Satan continues to attempt to confuse and question the absolute truth. For example, even in the last instance, there are those who attempt to question what the word "die" really means, including physical death and/or spiritual (death or separation from God).

To the delight of Satan, Christianity (salvation) and even the term "religion" has developed into a *philosophy* of man, though it is actually an *act* of God. By not fully understanding Scripture, man has fallen into Satan's trap. Thus, mankind fails to understand the purposes and intent of God's Word. All one has to do is look around at the various denominations and types of faith to see that things just do not fit. There is a cafeteria mentality in that people pick and choose their religious beliefs. They have an abundance of thoughts and ideas concerning God and salvation, but they never really understand the true nature of God or His plan. There is never a central truth or foundation from which to base a religious faith. Most often, people become inoculated with "a little of this and a little of that," and thus they cannot fully comprehend God's Word when they are exposed to the real thing.

In addition, there is the disease of "me," where current thoughts and beliefs emphasize man (not God). For many, their faith seems to urge them to either choose God or Satan. This mentality has a major flaw. This would mean that God and Satan both have votes, and you cast the deciding vote. This would make God equal with Satan and you equal with God! Thus, one's faith becomes what man has defined and not what God has ordained. The Bible seeks to make sure that train of thought is not true. The concepts of sin, true love, grace, and salvation all have biblical origins.

Many have said that unless you know the God of the Old Testament, you cannot know Jesus of the New Testament. Although the central thesis of the Bible is the nature of God (including Jesus), the expression of His nature is presented in different themes. It reveals God as a personality. Love and hate are two sides of the same coin. I *love* my wife but *hate* things that may harm her. God *loves* His creation but *hates* sin that can harm it. The God that we think is in the Scriptures is indeed the God of love but balanced with a God of justice.

The personality of God loves.

Certainly, as one reflects upon the person and character of God, the belief that "God is a God of love" would seem to be a major theme. And to an extent, this would be true. The Scripture is explicit in depicting God as a God of love. "For God so loved the world that He gave His only begotten son" (John 3:16). "As the father has loved me, so have I loved you" (John 15:9). "Love one another as I have loved you" (John 15:12). Therefore, one of the first personality or characteristic of God is that He loves.

The personality of God hates.

As an initial view of the person of God is that of love, it would seem that a characteristic of God would not include that of hate. However, Scripture says otherwise. "These six things does the Lord hate, yea seven are an abomination to him: a proud look, a lying tongue, hands that shed innocent blood, a heart that devises wicked imaginations, feet that be swift in running in mischief, a false witness that speaks lies and he that sows discord among brethren" (Proverbs 6:16–19).

"Hate the evil, love the good, and establish judgment at the gate" (Amos 5:15)

"All their wickedness is in Gilgal: for there I hated them: for the wickedness of their doing I will drive the out of my house, I will love them no more: all their princes are revolters" (Hosea 9:15).).

Therefore, in addition to having a loving personality, there are things God can and does hate.

The personality of God judges.

Of course if one holds the view that there is " a right or a wrong," one must also hold the view that there must be an authority of right and wrong, and that there must be "someone" who can "judge" what is right and what is wrong. Included within the personality of God is the view that since He created and "made the rules, He has the right to judge.

"And the Heavens shall declare his righteousness: for God is Judge Himself" (Psalms 50:6).

"But we are sure that the judgment of God is according to the truth against them which commit such things" (Romans 2:3).

Some "religions" have "salvation" in which going to Heaven is attained by doing good deeds. Some may say, "Yeah, I may do some bad things, but if I just do a lot of good things then the bad things can just be forgotten." Consider this. Suppose one of your parents or your wife or some other close relative or friend was murdered by someone. The perpetrator was tried and convicted in a court of law (based on the evidence and the law). However, the presiding judge proclaimed that because the perpetrator had also done some good things, he should be set free. Of course this should not be the "judgment" handed down by the judge. A judge cannot abdicate or abandon the law! By virtue of God's position as creator, including laws defining what is right and wrong, the Scripture is clear in stating that a personality of God is that of a Judge, adhering to the law.

The personality of God cares.

Many have said that God is a God who really does not care. He created and now just sits back and watches how things "work out". Yet God really does care, and the Scripture says it.

> "Casting all your cares on Him for He cares" (1 Peter 5:7).
> "Does God take care for oxen?" (1 Corinthians 9:9).
> "Are not two sparrows sold for a farthing? And one of them shall not fall on the ground without your Father." (Matthew 10:29.)

There is a song titled "His Eye Is On The Sparrow", written by Civilla D. Martin in 1905. The first verse and chorus is as follows:

Why should I be discouraged and why should the shadows fall?
Why should my heart be lonely and long for heaven and home?
When Jesus is my portion, my constant Friend is He,
His eye is on the sparrow and I know He watches me.
His eye is on the sparrow and I know He watches me.

I sing because I'm happy;
I sing because I'm free;
His eye is on the sparrow
And I know He watches me.

If an Almighty God takes care of all of His creation including the oxen and sparrow, surely how much do you think He cares for us?

The personality of God grieves.

Many "bad" things occur in everyday life including weather, traffic and disease tragedies. And it would seem discouraging to know that in spite of all "the good" that you seem to do, bad things still occur, including severe punishment and even death.

"And it repented the Lord that He had made man on the earth, and it grieved Him at his heart" (Genesis 6:6).

"And when he looked round about on them with anger, being grieved for the hardness of their hearts, he (Jesus) said unto the man. Stretch forth your hand. And he stretched it out: and his hand was restored whole as the other" (Mark 3:5).

"As Jesus drew near to the city of Jerusalem he wept over it saying, If you had known, even you, especially in this your day, the things that make for your peace. But now they are hidden from your eyes. For the days will come when your enemies will build an embankment around you, surround you and close you in on every side and level you and your children to the ground; and they will not leave in you one stone upon another, because you did not know the time of your visitation" (Luke 19: 41-44).

The personality of God does love, yet can hate. The personality of God does care yet can dispense judgment. And when things are not "well" with us, God cares enough to grieve.

Therefore, the Bible uses sixty-six books, penned by forty authors over a period of 1,500 years to describe Himself, His nature, and His purpose. No other text can come close to such. And although others could express their own ideas and impressions of the Bible, God's message of the Bible can be summed up in seven basic "themes." These include the following:

1. Who Is God?
2. What Is Sin?
3. Judgment of Sin
4. Redemption
5. Jesus: Son of God, Savior, and Redeemer
6. Books of the Bible: Revealing Jesus
7. There Was a Beginning, and There Will Be an End.

1. Who Is God?

As the personality of God unfolds in the Bible, the Bible illustrates that there is but one God!

He Is God

How would one define "a god"? What is a god. It is interesting to study the ancient pagan "gods" including the Greek or Roman "gods". In every case, there is not "One" god, or an "Ultimate" god, or a "god" that was (and still is) above all things. The God of the Bible describes such a god. The Bible depicts a God in whom there is no equal, or even close to being equal. The God of the Bible was not "created" by someone or something else. It was He who created all things. Therefore, by the definition as laid out by Scripture, the question is not "what" is god (or a god), but rather who is God. God is a person. He is a being that has no equal!

"In the beginning God created the heavens and he earth" (Genesis 1:1).

Although the God of the Bible is almighty and great enough to create the world, he is still personal enough to love, care and interact among His creation, including man.

"And I will walk among you, and will be your God, and you shall be my people. I am the Lord your God" (Leviticus 26:12–13). Therefore, one of the first tasks of the Bible is to present information that there is a god, and this god can be identified and recognized.

He Is Lord God

Although by definition as to who or what "God" means, man still has a difficult time defining absolute (as in an absolute god). Man has issues with defining an absolute truth, absolute love, absolute hate, absolute authority. The God of the Bible is absolute, regardless of our views or thoughts. Unfortunately, man must be told and reminded of this. Thus comes the expression "Lord God". There is but one God. And this means that although the very meaning and concept of "God" implies that there is no equal, our minds must be reminded of this. He is God of the world, including you and me. He is not just a God but the God...including your God and my God. Therefore, the Bible expresses this in the phrase "Lord God".

"These are the generation of the heavens and the earth when they were created in the day, in the day that the Lord God made the earth and the heavens" (Genesis 2:4).

"Unto you it was showed, that you might know that the Lord he is God; there is none else beside him" (Deuteronomy 4:35).

He Is the Living God

Most of man's pagan past includes attempting to "personify" their god. Thus statues and images were physically made with material such as stone or metals. Then the imagination of man had to create the "life" for that god. However, the God of the Bible has no statue or image depicting a god. The God of the Bible is described in real terms, as living being. He always has been living and He always will be living.

"And Joshua said, Hereby you shall know that the living God is among you" (Joshua 3:10). "I am the living bread which came down from heaven: if any man eat of this bread, he shall live forever: and the bread that I give is my flesh, which I give for the life of the world" (John 6:51). These Scriptures not only express that there is a God, but defines this God as a real living entity.

He Is Most High God

"And Melchizedek; king of Salem brought forth bread and wine: and he was priest to the Most High God" (Genesis 14:18).

"Though the Lord be high, yet he has respect for the lowly: but the proud he knows from afar off" (Psalms 138:6).

Thus, this "position" of God should not be taken lightly. By virtue of being God, there is no higher position.

He Is Almighty God

"And when Abram was ninety years old and nine, the Lord appeared unto him, I am the Almighty God, walk before me and be perfect" (Genesis 17:1).

"You have shown loving kindness unto thousands, and recompensed the iniquity of the fathers into the bosom of their children after them: Great, the Mighty God, the Lord of hosts, is his name" (Jeremiah 32:18).

It is because of what God does that makes Him Almighty. The fact that He is God makes Him almighty, but it is also what He does that makes Him almighty.

He Is Everlasting God

Man is limited by time and space, but God is not. God is not bound by time. "And Abraham planted a grove in Beersheba, and called there on the name of the Lord, the everlasting God" (Genesis 21:33).

"The eternal God is your refuge" (Deuteronomy 33:27).

"For this God is our God for ever and ever: he will be our guide even unto death" (Psalms 48:14).

God Is Spirit

Of course man is limited by time and space because man is physical. God is not bound by time or space because He is Spirit. "God is a spirit and they that worship him must worship Him in spirit and in truth" (John 4: 24).

"The grace of the Lord Jesus Christ [the Son] and the love of God [the Father] and the communion of the Holy Spirit be with you all" (2 Corinthians 13:14).

"Yet God is one God. He is One. Hear O Israel: The Lord our God is one Lord" (Deuteronomy 6:4).

God Is Infinite

Since God is Spirit and not defined by the physical, He is infinite. "But will God indeed dwell on the earth? Behold, the Heaven and heaven of heavens cannot contain you; how much less this house [the temple] that I have built" (1 Kings 8:27).

God Is Omnipotent or All-Powerful

What god could be God if God were not All-Powerful, All-Present, and All-knowing. "Ah, Lord God! Behold, you have made the heaven and the earth by your great power and stretched out arm, and there is nothing too hard for you. Behold, I am the Lord, the God of all flesh: is there anything too hard for me?" (Jeremiah 32:17, 27)

God Is Omnipresent or All-Present

"Whither shall I go from your Spirit? Or whither shall I flee from your presence? If I ascend up to heaven, you are there: if I make my bed in hell, behold you are there. If I take my wings of the morning, and dwell in the uttermost parts of the sea; even there shall your hand lead me, and your right hand shall hold me. If I say, Surely the darkness shall cover me; even the night shall be light about me. Yea, the darkness hides not from you, but the night shines as the day: the darkness and the light are both alike to you" (Psalms 139:7–12).

God Is Omniscience or All-Knowing

"Or if our heart condemns us, God is greater than our heart, and knows all things" (1 John 3:20).

God Is Righteous

Having defined that God is Almighty and Spirit and not bound by the physical, and that he is All-Powerful, All-Present and All-knowing, He is also defined as being Righteous, Perfect and Holy.

"The Lord is righteous in all his ways, and holy in all his works" (Psalms 145:17).

God Is Perfect

"As for God, his way is perfect; the word of the Lord is tried: he is a buckler to all of those that trust him" (Psalms 18:30).

God Is Holy

"Holy, Holy, Holy, Lord God Almighty which was, and is and is to come" (Revelation 4:8).

These expressions describing God are only the tip of the iceberg. But again, it is amazing that throughout the time frame of the writing of the Bible, God is still described in similar terms.

2. What Is Sin?

As the personality of God becomes manifest, it becomes apparent that as a holy, perfect God, the person of God cannot associate with sin. Thus, it would make sense that within the text of the Bible, there should be a definition of sin.

It is amazing that what used to be (considered) sin is no longer (considered) sin by man. However, the definition of sin has never changed throughout the Bible, according to the Word of God.

Sin Is Transgression of the Law (of God)

"Whosoever commits sin transgresses also the law; for sin is the transgression of the law" (1 John 3:4).

Sin Is Unbelief

"He that believes on the Son of God has the witness in himself: he that believes not God has made God a liar; because he believes not the record that God gave His Son" (1 John 5:10).

Sin Is Active and Passive Rebellion against God

"Hear O heavens, and give ear, O earth: for the Lord has spoken, I have nourished and brought up children, and they have rebelled against me" (Isaiah 1:2).

Sin Is Unrighteousness

"All unrighteousness is sin: and there is a sin not unto death" (1 John 5:17).

The Origin of Sin

Any discussion of the origin of sin must begin with the origin itself, or Satan, also known as Lucifer. He was created as an angel, not as Satan (the Deceiver). "And God saw every thing that he had made and behold, it was very good" (Genesis 1:31). Thus, God did not create evil. "God dwells in holiness, not a place of evil. God reigns over the heathen: God sits upon the throne of his holiness" (Psalms 47:8).

In an iconic example describing the king of Babylon, God was able to describe the very person of Lucifer or Satan as the author of sin.

> How you have fallen from heaven, O Lucifer, son of the morning! How you are cut down to the ground, which did weaken the nations! For you have said in your heart, I will ascend into the heaven, I will exalt my throne above the stars of God: I will sit also upon the mount of the congregation, in the sides of the north: I will ascend above the heights of the clouds; I will be like the most High. (Isaiah 14: 12–14)

Lucifer had previously led a rebellion of sorts before the time of the Garden of Eden. "And there was war in heaven; and Michael and his angels fought against the dragon; and the dragon fought and his angels and prevailed not; neither was their place found anymore in heaven. And the great dragon was cast out, that old serpent, called the Devil, and Satan, which deceives the whole world: he was cast out into the earth, and his angels were cast out with him" (Revelation 12:7–9). "For God spared not the angels that sinned but cast them down to hell, and to be delivered into chains of darkness, to be reserved unto judgment" (1 Peter 2:4).

There can be no doubt that the former angel Lucifer, whom we now speak of as Satan, is the originator of sin, but even Satan and the other fallen angels cannot escape God's ultimate judgment. "Then he shall say unto them on the left hand, Depart from me, you cursed, into everlasting fire, prepared for the devil and his angels" (Matthew 25:41).

In addition, there can be no doubt that any and all sin, regardless of origin or nature will be judged and that those found guilty will be condemned.

The fall of man is found in Genesis 3 (Old Testament). When Adam sinned, his seed became corrupt. And this is even stated in Romans (New Testament):

> For therein is the righteousness of God revealed from faith to faith: as it is written, The just shall live by faith. [This is a quote from Habakkuk 2:4.] For the wrath of God is revealed from heaven against all ungodliness and unrighteousness of men, who hold back the truth in unrighteousness; because that which may be known of God is manifest in them; for God has showed it to them (man). For the invisible things of him from the creation of the world are clearly seen, being understood by the things that are made, even his eternal power and Godhead; so that they are without excuse: because that, when they (man) knew God, they glorified him not as God, neither were thankful; but became vain in their imaginations, and their foolish heart was darkened. Professing themselves to be wise, they are fools, and changed the glory of the incorruptible God into an image made like to corruptible man, and to birds, and four-footed beasts, and creeping things. (Romans 2:17–23)

Thus, corruptible seed produces corruptible nature. "A good tree cannot bring forth evil fruit, neither can a corrupt tree bring forth good fruit" (Matthew 7:18).

Therefore, man is born with a sinful nature and cannot deny or escape this. "For all have sinned and come short of the glory of God" (Romans 3:23). This may be the most "semi" quoted verse in the Bible as many justify their sinful actions by saying, "Well, nobody's perfect!" Man is not a sinner because he sins. Man sins because he is a sinner. Thus, the problem is that it is man's nature to not be good, although many may say that they try to see the good in people. To be sure, in our eyes, we can indeed do good. Simply witness the acts of goodness following natural disasters like hurricanes, tornadoes, etc. But we still sin.

Sin carries a barbed hook. Satan has baited the hook, and we bite. Satan then keeps you on the line longer than you really expected ... maybe too long, maybe to the end. The bait "looks good." Of course, that is the intent. The Bible even speaks to this. According to Genesis 3:6, Eve was tempted (baited) by the good looks of the fruit. "And when the woman saw that the tree was good and that it was pleasant to the eyes, and a tree to be desired to make one wise, she took of the fruit thereof and did eat." Later in Genesis 13:10–11, Abraham and Lot part ways. Lot was also tempted (baited) as he chose to go toward Sodom and Gomorrah to live because it "looked good."

> And Lot lifted up his eyes, and beheld all the plain of Jordan, that it was well watered every where, before the Lord destroyed Sodom and Gomorrah, even as the garden before the Lord, like the land of Egypt, as you come to Zoar. Then Lot chose him all the plain of Jordan; and Lot Journeyed east: and they (Abraham and Lot) separated themselves the one from another.

Thus, as one "studies" the Bible, whether the material directly concerns God, sin, anything, one understands that even the exact wording of the text is so eloquently expressed that it gives a deeper meaning and understanding of what an almighty, omnipotent, infinite God is trying to convey to a sinful, finite, mortal man. And no sinful, finite, mortal man is capable of penning such a text!

Because God is holy and without sin, He cannot, therefore, by His own nature, associate with man because of the sin of man. When God originally created man, He created man in a perfect state ... without sin. But man, because of his sin, lost this perfect state and the perfect relationship with the perfect God. And because man lost this perfect state, there are consequences for sin.

3. Judgment of Sin

There must be a judgment for sin. One cannot sin and get away with it. There are consequences. Many times individuals may express a desire to forgive and forget, without recognizing that there must be a price paid for that sin. Because God is holy and righteous and thus cannot associate with sin, a carrier of sin is subject to the results of sin.

"For the wages of sin is death" (Romans 6:23). The Bible teaches that death is not "the end." Death is a spiritual separation. The sins literally separate one from God. Thus, there's the expression "you are 'dead' to your sins." Death is a physical separation as it separates the spirit and soul from the body. Finally, death is eternal. Sin will separate "the carrier" from the presence of God forever.

"But we are sure that the judgment of God is according to truth against them which commit such things" (Romans 2:2). "And the heavens shall declare his righteousness; for God is judge himself" (Psalm 50:6). "And Jesus said, For judgment I am come into this world, that they which see not might see; and they which see might be made blind" (John 9:39).

Of course, the purpose of a trial is not just to pronounce "judgment" but to place evidence in the balance. If the evidence falls to "guilty," then the judgment follows. Because God is perfect, one sin can prevent presence with Him. Only one! God has to judge sin to make us aware that there is sin and that we are guilty of it. At one time, man was perfect, but not now. However, by God's redemptive plan, our sinful state of death can triumph in His glory.

We all like a nice arrangement of cut flowers. On Valentine's Day, women like to receive roses. At funerals, the beautiful floral sprays and pleasing displays can help ease the pain and sorrow of loss. However, it is ironic that these flowers are already dead! In a similar sense, our sins have already made us dead. We may think we are alive as we see ourselves as beautiful flowers in our own light. But the reality is that we are already dead, and it is just a matter of a short time when we will actually be able to see that. It is God that needs to be seen. Thus we are actually the pot from which the real, live flower emerges and grows. That is God *in* us. Because of God, we can be made alive, but not be the cut, dead flower that comes back alive, but we can be the pot from which the flower can grow. In other words, we are not the flower. We are the pot from which sprouts and grows God's glory (a real living flower)! This is the contrast in judgment. We are either already dead, or God's glory grows from us. And it can be seen by us and through us.

Another analogy is a glove. We may discuss and describe how pretty or how warm a glove may be, but it is the hand (of a living being) that really matters. We are only the glove. We are nothing of value until the hand is performing its function through the glove. We are the glove and God that is *in* us performs the deeds.

"And you shall swear, The Lord lives, in truth, in judgment, and in righteousness; and in the nations shall bless themselves in him, and in him shall they glory" (Jeremiah 4:2).

4. Redemption

Although the Bible describes the person of God and the nature of sin, it can be said that the Bible is really a book of redemption. The verb "redeem" means to reclaim or recover or repossess. Thus, the idea of "redemption" is twofold. It refers to a fallen state (for some reason) and the ransom or deliverance and returning to the former (unfallen) state. In Genesis, we find that man lost the perfect state because his will was contrary to God's will. He did that which God told him not to do. In other words, man sinned. If there were immediate judgment in this circumstance, man would stand condemned, guilty of sin. Man would be unable to "buy back" by his own nature and reclaim that perfect, sinless state. But God was able to "buy back" this perfect, sinless state. However, there was a tremendous price... His only begotten son, Jesus.

Also in Genesis, we see that redemptive process. Jesus is the seed of the woman that will defeat Satan, the author of sin. "And I will put enmity between thee and the woman, and between thy seed and her seed; it shall bruise thy head, and thou shall bruise his heel" (Genesis 3:15).

At the beginning when man sinned, man tried to cover up using a fig leaf. This cover was unacceptable. God had to sacrifice animals (shed perfect, innocent blood) in order to clothe man (Adam and Eve). "Wherefore, as one by one man sin entered into the world, and death by sin; and so death passed upon all men, for that all have sinned: For until the law sin was in the world: but sin is not imputed when there is no law. Nevertheless death reigned from Adam to Moses, even over them that had sinned after the likeness of Adam's transgression, who is the figure of him that was to come" (Romans 5: 12–14).

So God's plan of salvation was redemption, the "buying back" with the ultimate, innocent blood ... of Jesus. The book of Ruth best explains the concept of redemption ... of things lost but no regained. In fact, there is a scarlet (blood) trail throughout the entire Old

Testament into the New Testament in the person of God (the Son). Because God is righteous, perfect, and holy, He cannot associate with sin. That is His nature. Man, on the other hand, is not a sinner because we sin, but we sin because we are sinners.

If sin is transgression of the law of God and is unrighteousness, how then can we ascribe to being perfect? The answer is we cannot. "Therefore being justified by faith we have peace with God through our Lord Jesus Christ ... Wherefore, as by one man (Adam) entered the world, and death by sin, and so death passed upon all men, for that all have sinned: (For until the law sin was in the world: but sin is not imputed when there is no law. Nevertheless, death reigned from Adam to Moses" (Romans 5:12–14). "For sin shall not have dominion over you: for you are not under the law, but under grace" (Romans 6:14). Certainly if we rob a bank, we are guilty of a crime and deserve punishment. Scripture is clear that when man sinned and became unrighteous, that sin separated man from God and the punishment is death. That is where God intervened. And this intervention was planned from the beginning!

"There is therefore now no condemnation to them which are in Christ Jesus, who walk not after flesh, but after the Spirit. For the law of the Spirit of life in Christ Jesus has made me free from the law of sin and death. For what the law could not do, in that it was weak through the flesh, God sending his own Son in the likeness of sinful flesh, and for sin, condemned sin in the flesh: That the righteousness of the law might be fulfilled in us, who walk not after the flesh, but after the Spirit" (Romans 8:1–4). Jesus said, "Think not that I am come to destroy the law, or the prophets: I am not come to destroy, but to fulfill" (Matthew 5:17).

Through man's sin, death entered the world. We lost our perfect state (in creation) back in the Garden of Eden. Thus, to "regain" our perfect state, the cost of losing it has to be repaid. This "repayment" concept is called redemption. God's redemptive plan of salvation (leading up to the death of Jesus on the cross and the resurrection from the garden tomb) is woven throughout Scripture.

Imagine gravity. We are subject to the effects of gravity. We fall off of a ladder, and we "plummet" to the ground because of gravity. We drop a coin from our hand, and the coin falls to the floor because of gravity.

The coin has no choice but to succumb to the effects of gravity. Now imagine again that coin falling, but then picture a hand reaching out and preventing the coin from falling and hitting the floor. So it is with redemption and our salvation. There are laws describing what sin is, and because of our physical (human) nature, we are subject to those laws. As a result, we fall. However, through redemption, the "hand of God" reaches out and catches us so that we do not "hit the floor" and die.

This "process" comes from the book of Genesis to the book of the Revelation by forty different authors over a 1,500 year period ... and it all matches! Even Jesus said, "Search the scriptures (i.e., Old Testament); for in them you think you have eternal life: and they are they which testify of me ... For if you believed Moses, you would have believed me: for he wrote of me. But if you believe not his writings how shall you believe my words" (John 5:39, 46–7). Thus, following the fact there is a real, named God, the rest of Scripture is an expose on redemption, what redemption is, where it came from, and how it is to be received.

5. Jesus: Son of God, Savior, and Redeemer

For many, good works are crucial to salvation and "entry to heaven." However, the Bible is clear that is not the case. "You believe that there is one God; you do well: the demons also believe and tremble" (James 2:19). Interestingly, nowhere does the Bible attempt to prove or even argue the existence of God. The existence of God is simply taken for granted, and a universal belief of "a god" comes from within man. But the Bible does lay out the existence, nature, and need of Jesus Christ, the Redeemer and Savior of man (from the judgment of his sins).

> Brethren, my heart's desire and prayer to God for Israel is, that they might be saved. For I bear them record that they have a zeal of God, but not according knowledge. For they being ignorant of God's righteousness, and going about to establish their own righteousness have not submitted themselves unto the righteousness of God. For Christ is the end of the law for righteousness to everyone that believes. (Romans 10:1–4)

Someone once said that it was better that Jesus walked on the earth than man walked on the moon. Jesus is our Redeemer, our salvation from judgment of our sins. Toward the very beginning of the Bible in the Old Testament, we see the story of the cross (found later in the Bible in the New Testament) and the story of Abraham as he (Abraham) is willing to sacrifice his son, Isaac. But God provides for Himself a ram (sacrifice) for a substitute.

> And Abraham said, My son, God will provide himself a lamb for a burnt offering: so they went both of them together ... And Abraham stretched forth his hand, and took the knife to slay his son. The angel of the Lord called unto him out of heaven, and said, Abraham, Abraham: and he said Here am I. And he said, Lay not your hand upon the lad, neither do any thing unto him: for now I know that you fear God, seeing you have not withheld you son, your only son from me. And Abraham lifted up his eyes, and looked, and behold behind him a ram caught in a thicket by his horns: and Abraham went and took the ram, and offered him up for a burnt offering in place of his son. (Genesis 22:8, 10–13)

In Exodus, we see the cross in the Passover Lamb. "When I see the blood, I will Passover you" (Exodus 12:13).

In Leviticus, we see the (blood) sacrifice of the cross. "For the life of the flesh is in the blood: and I have given it to you upon the altar to make atonement for your souls: for it is the blood that makes atonement for the soul" (Leviticus 17:11).

In Numbers, we see the cross when Moses lifted up the serpent in the wilderness. "And as Moses lifted up the snake in the desert, so the son of man must be lifted up" (John 3:14).

In Deuteronomy of the Old Testament and 1 Corinthians and Luke in the New Testament, we see the cross in the smitten rock and the manna.

> Who led you through that great and terrible wilderness wherein were fiery serpents, scorpions and drought, where there was no water, who brought you water out of the rock of flint; Who fed

> you in the wilderness with manna which your fathers knew not, that he might humble you, and that he might prove you to do good at the later end. (Deuteronomy 8:15–16)

> Moreover, brethren, I would not that you be ignorant, how that our fathers were under the cloud, and all passed through the sea; and were all baptized unto Moses in the cloud and in the sea; and did eat the same spiritual meat; and did all drink the same spiritual drink: for they drank of that spiritual Rock that followed them: and that Rock was Christ. And all did drink the same spiritual drink. (1 Corinthians 10:1-4)

Consider Luke 22:19: "And he (Jesus) took the bread and gave thanks, and brake it, and gave it to them saying, This is my body which is given for you: this do in remembrance of me."

John 1:1 says, "In the beginning was the Word, and the Word was with God, and the Word was God." And John 1:14 goes on to say, "And the Word was made flesh, and dwelt among us, (and we beheld his glory, the glory as of the only begotten of the Father,) full of grace and truth."

In the Old Testament writing in Numbers 24:17, we read, "I shall see him, but not now: I shall behold him, but not nigh: there shall come a Star out of Jacob, and a Scepter shall rise out of Israel, and shall smite the corners of Moab, and destroy all the children of Sheth." And in the New Testament book of Acts, we find, "To him give all the prophets witness, that through his name whosoever believes in him shall receive remission of sins" (Acts 10:43).

Thus, the trail of Jesus Christ as God and Savior can be followed throughout the Bible. The Bible is not just about God but the person of God expressed through Jesus Christ. However, even the Bible mentions those who will not believe. "Enter in at the strait gate: for wide is the gate, and broad is the way, that leads to destruction, and many there be which go thereat; because strait is the gate, and narrow is the way which leads unto life, and few there be that find it" (Matthew 7:13–14).

6. Books of the Bible: Revealing Jesus

The Bible is clear in describing God as so almighty, so all-powerful that He can create and that He can take care of His creation. Not only did He create the spiritual, He also created the physical. He loves His creation, including man. He is also righteous and holy and without blemish. When Satan introduced sin (even before the creation of man), God had to separate Himself from sin. When man sinned, man was separated from the perfect state in which he was created.

But in His omnipotence and infinite wisdom and foreknowledge, God was able to demonstrate His power over sin (and subsequent death) through His love by creating a "plan of salvation" (at the time of His initial creation). There certainly was not a situation that God created and then Satan entered the scene and "messed" things up so that God had to quickly devise a "scheme" to "salvage" His creation. His plan of salvation was established from the very beginning. That plan of salvation was literally giving Himself as our sacrifice.

Thus, the story of who God is and what He has done had to be conveyed to man, but in a form and manner that man could understand. This story took 1,500 years and forty plus God-inspired authors of different backgrounds to tell it "ironically" in what we call the Bible. God is committed to His creation! He created it and "recaptured" it or redeemed it (in a perfect state once again). As one ponders the term "commitment," consider the following question: Which is greater? The cost of making a commitment or the cost of keeping it?

There is a story of commitment. A boy was born to a young man and woman in Mexico. During birth, the young mother died. The father made a commitment to raise his son and to always be there for him. It was not long before his "commitment" was tested. In 1985, there was a major earthquake in Mexico City. The elementary school where this man's son attended was heavily damaged. The father rushed to the scene only to find the school building had totally collapsed ... onto the students who were inside. The father began to dig with his bare hands, pulling bricks and debris from the rubble. Rescue workers said, "Back away. It's no use. You can't do that alone."

Twelve hours passed, and the father was still digging, removing the heavy bricks and twisted steel with his bare hands. The firemen said, "Stop. We will help." But they were too busy with other areas of the disaster. Twenty-four hours passed, and the father was still digging. His hands were cut and bleeding.

Curious passersby railed, "It's no use. Please stop!"

But the young father diligently kept digging. Thirty-six hours had passed. The father kept digging and calling out for his son until … he finally heard the faint voice of his son. "Dad, we are here. We are safe!"

The father was elated. Emotionally and physically drained, the father said, "Here, Son, I will get you out."

"No, Father," his son replied. "There are eleven of us here. Get them out first. I knew you would come for me!" In the young father's commitment to his own son, he had literally saved ten other children.

There is another story illustrating what commitment means. Of course, during the Vietnam War in the late 1960s and early 70s, there was a lot of killing and bloodshed. All the members of the eleven-year-old boy's family were killed except for his eight-year-old sister. But she was in bad shape and desperately needed blood. The young boy volunteered, but the American nurses were reluctant because of his young age. But they decided to get just a little blood, hoping to help the girl and buy her some time for better treatment without compromising the health of the boy. After a few moments during the transfusion, the boy began to sniffle as he began to cry. The nurse, thinking that the needle was just hurting his arm, asked compassionately, "Does it hurt?"

"No," the boy replied, "I was just wondering what it was going to be like when I die."

The nurse began to cry. The young lad actually thought he was going to die by donating some of his blood, but by his choice, the nurse understood that he was willing to do just that for his sister.

God knows full well what the act of commitment means. He gave Himself (Jesus) for payment of our sins. As such, Jesus (and what He represents) is indeed mentioned in every book of the Bible, fitly framing together and tying together the entire Bible.

So how can we describe the nature of God? God created, and His Word said of it that "it was very good" (Genesis 1:31). But what does that really mean? God chose to create the physical in order to describe His power, righteousness, mercy, and judgment. There are collectively sixty-six books of the Bible, each describing in harmony the nature of God and showing Jesus. Other writings (of man) simply describe "how one should live his or her life" or other rules and regulations of living. However, God's Word describes much more, and His Word is set apart from man's word.

Because man is physical, our senses are used to guide and drive our very being. We are surrounded with various images or icons. We can easily identify the meaning of these instant "pictures." Business icons advertise their products ... and we recognize them. Computers, iPhones, or other electronic devices use icons to help us understand how to use the computer applications. For example, we see a picture of a truck with a circle around it and a line through it. This sign means "no trucks allowed." Humans need icons or pictures that we can identify with in our physical world. As a good exercise, one can describe a beautiful sunset to a blind man! So it is with God. So it is with the writing of the Bible. How could He best describe His nature to His crowning creation—man? God understood this long before He created man. The Bible is full of icons, stories, occurrences, and circumstances that as humans, we can better understand and relate.

From the beginning of the Bible in the book of Genesis to the end of the Bible in the book of the Revelation, Jesus is often shown as the expression of God's heart.

He Is the Promise that Breaks the Curse

"And unto Adam he said, Because you have harkened unto the voice of your wife, and have eaten of the tree, of which I commanded you saying, you shall not eat of it: cursed is the ground for you sake: in sorrow shall you eat of it all the days of your life" (Genesis 3:17). "You are cursed with a curse: for you have robbed me, even the whole nation" (Malachi 3:9). His body shall not remain all night upon the tree, but you shall in any wise bury him that day; (for he that is hanged is accursed of God); that your land be not defiled, which the Lord your God gives you for an inheritance" (Deuteronomy 21:23). "Christ has redeemed us from the curse of the law, being made a curse for us: for it is written, Cursed is every one that hangs on a tree" (Galatians 3:13). "And there shall be no more curse: but the throne of God and of the lamb shall be in it; and his servants shall serve him" (Revelation 22:3).

He Is the Promised Son to Eve

"I will put enmity between you (Satan) and the woman, and between your seed and her seed; and it shall bruise you head and you shall bruise his heel" (Genesis 3:15). "And the devil that deceived them was cast into the lake of fire and brimstone, where the beast and the false prophet are, and shall be tormented day and night for ever and ever" (Revelation 20:10).

He Is the Atonement Cover on the Ark

"For that day shall the priest make an atonement for you, to cleanse you. That you may be clean before the Lord" (Leviticus 16:30). "But Christ, being come a high priest of good things to come, by a greater more perfect tabernacle, not made with hands, that is to say, not of this building; neither by the blood of goats and calves, but by his own blood he entered in once into the holy place, having obtained eternal redemption for us" (Hebrews 9:11–12). "So Christ was once offered to bear the sins of many" (Hebrews 9:28).

He Is the Bridegroom

"He that has the bride is the bridegroom: but the friend of the bridegroom, which stands and hears him, rejoices greatly because the bridegroom's voice: this my joy therefore is fulfilled" (John 3:29).

"And I heard as it were the voice of a great multitude, and as the voice of mighty thundering, saying, Alleluia: for the Lord God omnipotent reigns. Let us be glad and rejoice, and give honor to him: for the marriage of the Lamb is come and his wife has made herself ready. And to was granted that she should be arrayed in fine linen, clean and white: for the fine linen is the righteousness of saints" (Revelation 19:6–8).

He Is the Burning Bush

> And Moses said, I will now turn aside, and see this great sight, why the bush is not burnt. And when the Lord saw that he turned aside to see, God called unto him out of the midst of the bush, and said, Moses, Moses, and he said here am I. And he said put off your shoes from your feet for the place whereon you stand is holy ground. Moreover he said I am (the God of Abraham) ... I am come down ... and God said to Moses, I am that I am. (Exodus 3:4–6, 8, 14)

What a strange sight that must have been...A burning bush that was not being consumed. Although we may not understand the entire Bible, it certainly can grab our attention and captivate us with its words.

"I am Alpha and Omega, the beginning and the end, the first and the last" (Revelation 22:13). "Jesus said unto them, verily, verily I say unto you, Before Abraham was, I am" (John 8:58). But regardless how one may view the Bible, God's creation and Word have been deliberately developed and presented to man. There are other "analogies" of God's word and its meaning to man. On other occasions, Jesus said that He was the following:

- The bread of life (John 6:35)
- The light of the world (John 8:12)
- The door (John 10:9)
- The good shepherd (John 10:11)
- The resurrection (John 11:25)
- The way, the truth, the life (John 14:6)
- The true vine (John 15:1)

He Is the Sacrifice for Our Sins and Save Us

"For when we were yet without strength, in due time Christ died for the ungodly. For scarcely for a righteous man will one die; yet peradventure for a good man some would even dare to die. But God commended his love toward us, in that while we were yet sinners, Christ died for us. Much more then, being justified by his blood, we shall be saved, from wrath through him" (Romans 5:6–9).

As the Bible unfolds from Genesis to Revelation, descriptions, depictions and metaphors of Jesus can be seen.

- In Genesis, Jesus is the Ram at Abraham's altar.
- In Exodus, Jesus is the Passover Lamb.
- In Leviticus, Jesus is the High Priest.
- In Numbers, Jesus is the Cloud by day and the Pillar of Fire by night.
- In Deuteronomy, Jesus is the City of our refuge.
- In Joshua, Jesus is the Scarlet Thread out Rahab's window.
- In Judges, Jesus is our Judge.
- In Ruth, Jesus is our Kinsman Redeemer.
- In 1 and 2 Samuel, Jesus is our Trusted Prophet.
- In Kings and Chronicles, Jesus is our Reigning King.
- In Ezra, Jesus is our Faithful Scribe.
- In Nehemiah, Jesus is the Rebuilder of everything that is broken.
- In Esther, Jesus is Mordecai sitting faithfully at the gate.
- In Job, Jesus is our Redeemer that ever lives.
- In Psalms, Jesus is my Shepherd and I shall not want.

- In Proverbs and Ecclesiastes, Jesus is our Wisdom.
- In the Song of Solomon, Jesus is the Beautiful Bridegroom.
- In Isaiah, Jesus is the Suffering Servant.
- In Jeremiah and Lamentations, Jesus is the Weeping Prophet.
- In Ezekiel, Jesus the Wonderful Four-Faced Man.
- In Daniel, Jesus is the Fourth Man in the midst of a fiery furnace.
- In Hosea, Jesus is my Love that is forever faithful.
- In Joel, Jesus baptizes us with the Holy Spirit.
- In Amos, Jesus is our Burden Bearer.
- In Obadiah, Jesus is our Savior.
- In Jonah, Jesus is the Great Foreign Missionary that takes the Word of God into the entire world.
- In Micah, Jesus is the Messenger with beautiful feet.
- In Nahum, Jesus is the Avenger.
- In Habakkuk, Jesus is the Watchman that is ever-praying for revival.
- In Zephaniah, Jesus is the Lord mighty to save.
- In Haggai, Jesus is the Restorer of our lost heritage.
- In Zechariah, Jesus is our Fountain.
- In Malachi, Jesus is the Sun of Righteousness with healing in His wings.
- In Matthew, Jesus is the Christ, the Son of the Living God.
- In Mark, Jesus is the Miracle Worker.
- In Luke, Jesus is the Son of Man.

- In John, Jesus is the Door by which every one of us must enter.
- In Acts, Jesus is the Shining Light at appears to Saul on the road to Damascus.
- In Romans, Jesus is our Justifier.
- In 1 Corinthians, Jesus is our Resurrection.
- In 2 Corinthians, Jesus is our Sin Bearer.
- In Galatians, Jesus redeems (Redeemer) us from the law.
- In Ephesians, Jesus is our Unsearchable Riches.
- In Philippians, Jesus supplies (Sustainer) our every need.
- In Colossians, Jesus is the Fullness of the Godhead.
- In 1 and 2 Thessalonians, Jesus is our Soon Coming King.
- In 1 and 2 Timothy, Jesus is the Mediator between God and man.
- In Philemon, Jesus is a Friend that sticks closer than a brother.
- In Hebrews, Jesus is the Blood of the Everlasting Covenant.
- In James, Jesus is the Lord that heals the sick.
- In 1 and 2 Peter, Jesus is the Chief Shepherd.
- In 1, 2, and 3 John, it is Jesus who has the tenderness of love.
- In Jude, Jesus is the Lord coming with ten thousand saints.
- In Revelation, Jesus is the Lord of Lords and King of Kings, the Alpha and Omega, the Great *I Am*.

Not only is Jesus depicted in the Old Testament and the New Testament, but one can make connections between each. Jesus is referred to and talked about in the Old Testament, and these references come to fruition in the New Testament. Some may refer to these as "prophecies," as they are mentioned one place in the Bible and come true at a later date. There are more than a thousand fulfilled prophecies in the Bible. There are some 380 prophecies concerning Christ, forty-eight of which were fulfilled in the last week of His ministry. The following comparisons (or fulfillment of prophecies) of Christ are but a few examples. There are certainly more. No other texts come close to such connections.

- Jesus would be bruised, but He would crush the head of Satan (Genesis 3:15, Revelation 20:10).
- Jesus would be God (Zechariah 11:12–13, John 12:45).
- Jesus would be the Son of God (Psalm 2:7, 12; Matthew 17:5).
- Jesus would be the Seed of the Women (Genesis 3:15, Luke 1:34–5).
- Jesus would be a descendant (seed) of Abraham, Isaac, and Jacob (Genesis 12:3, 17:19, 28:14; Luke 3:23–4).
- Jesus would be a king in the line of Judah (Genesis 49:10, John 1:49).
- Jesus would be from the tribe of Judah (1 Chronicles 5:2, Luke 3:23–32).
- Jesus would be a descendant of David (Ezekiel 34:23–4, Matthew 1:1).
- Jesus would be proceeded by a forerunner (Isaiah 40:3, Luke 1:17).
- Jesus would be born in Bethlehem (Micah 5:2, Matthew 2:1–2).
- Jesus would be born of a virgin (Isaiah 7:14, Luke 1:34–5).
- Jesus would heal the blind, lame, deaf (Isaiah 35:5–6, Mark 10:51–2).

- Jesus would be hated without cause (Psalms 69:4, Luke 23:13–22).
- Jesus would be despised by the Jewish nation (Isaiah 49:7, John 10:20, Matthew 27:23).
- Jesus would be ride into Jerusalem on a donkey (Zechariah 9:9, Matthew 21:6–9).
- Jesus would be despised and crucified (Psalm 22:6–8, 14; Luke 23:21–3; Matthew 27:35).
- Jesus would be whipped and beaten (Isaiah 50:6; Matthew 26:67, 27:26).
- God would darken the day at noon during Jesus' death (Amos 8:9, Matthew 27:45–6).
- Jesus would be pierced (Zechariah 12:10, John 19:34–7).
- Jesus' death was foretold in Daniel (Daniel 9:26, John 19:30).
- Jesus would be resurrected (Psalms 16:8–10, Acts 13:30–7).
- Jesus would be resurrected and live forever (Isaiah 53:10, Mark 16:16).
- Jesus would be Lord, seated at the right hand of God (Psalms 110:1, 5; 1 Peter 3:21–2).

In addition to these fulfilled prophecies within the Bible, Jesus can be also be typified in the characters found in the Bible. These iconic images illustrate the truths about Jesus and can be seen in the following:

- In the books of Genesis, Matthew, Mark, Luke, and John, Jesus is typified in the life of Isaac, the sacrificed son.
- Also in the book of Genesis, Jesus is typified in the life of Joseph, the rejected brother.

- In the books of Exodus and Hebrews, Jesus is typified as the Passover lamb.
- Also in the book of Exodus and in the book of Romans, Jesus is typified in the life of Moses, the deliverer.
- Also in the book of Exodus and in the book of John, Jesus is typified as the manna (bread) from heaven.
- In the books of Exodus, Joshua, and Revelation, Jesus is typified as in the person of Joshua, the Captain of our Salvation and Commander of the Army.
- In the book of Leviticus, Jesus is typified in the sacrifices and offerings.
- Also in the book of Leviticus and in the book of Hebrews, Jesus is typified as the High Priest.
- In the books of Numbers and 1 Corinthians, Jesus is typified as the Rock.
- In the book of Deuteronomy, Jesus is typified as the Prophet.
- In the book of Judges, Jesus is typified as the Lawgiver and true Judge.
- In the book of Ruth, Jesus is typified in the person of Boaz, the Redeemer.
- In the book of 1 Samuel, Jesus is typified in the life of David the King (exile).
- In the book of 1 Samuel, Jesus is typified in the life of Jonathon, the faithful friend.
- In the books of Kings 1 and 2, Jesus is typified in the life of Solomon (the Millennial Reign).
- In the book of 2 Kings, Jesus is typified in the life and miracles of the prophet Elisha

- In the book of Ezra, Jesus is typified in the person of Zerubbabel, the rebuilder of the temple.
- In the book of Nehemiah Jesus is typified in the person of Nehemiah, rebuilder of the walls of salvation.
- In the book of Esther, Jesus is typified in the person of Mordecai (savior of the Jews).
- In the book of Job, Jesus is typified in the sufferings of Job and the blessings that would follow.

Therefore, after one studies these scriptures in the Old and New Testament, the person finds that each book of the Bible reveals the following about Jesus:

- In the book of Genesis, Jesus is the breath of life.
- In Exodus, Jesus is the Passover Lamb.
- In Leviticus, Jesus is our High Priest.
- In Numbers, Jesus is the fire by night.
- In Deuteronomy, Jesus is Moses' voice.
- In Joshua, Jesus is salvation's choice.
- In Judges, Jesus is the lawgiver.
- In Ruth, Jesus is the kinsmen-redeemer.
- In 1 and 2 Samuel, Jesus is our trusted prophet.
- In Kings and Chronicles, Jesus is sovereign.
- In Ezra, Jesus is true and faithful scribe.
- In Nehemiah, Jesus is the rebuilder of broken walls and lives.
- In Esther, Jesus is Mordecai's courage.
- In the book of Job, Jesus is the timeless redeemer.

- In the book of Psalms, Jesus is our morning song.
- In Proverbs, Jesus is wisdom's cry.
- In Ecclesiastes, Jesus is the time and season.
- In the Song of Solomon, Jesus is the lover's dream.
- In Isaiah, Jesus is Prince of Peace.
- In Jeremiah, Jesus is the weeping prophet.
- In Lamentations, Jesus is the cry for Israel.
- In Ezekiel, Jesus is the call from sin.
- In Daniel, Jesus is the stranger in the fire.
- In Hosea, Jesus is forever faithful.
- In Joel, Jesus is the Spirit's power.
- In Amos, He is the arms that carry us.
- In Obadiah, He is the Lord, our Savior.
- In Jonah, He is the great missionary.
- In Micah, He is the promise of peace.
- In Nahum, He is our strength and our shield.
- In Habakkuk and Zephaniah, He is pleading for revival.
- In Haggai, He restores a lost heritage.
- In Zechariah, He is our fountain.
- In Malachi, Jesus is the son of righteousness rising with healing in His wings.
- In Matthew, Mark, Luke, and John, He is God, man, and Messiah.

- In the book of Acts, He is fire from heaven.
- In Romans, He is the grace of God.
- In Corinthians, He is the power of love.
- In Galatians, He is freedom from the curse of sin.
- In Ephesians, He is our glorious treasure.
- In Philippians, He is the servant's heart.
- In Colossians, He is the Godhead Trinity.
- In Thessalonians, He is our coming King.
- In Timothy, Titus, and Philemon, He is our mediator and our faithful Pastor.
- In the book of Hebrews, He is the everlasting covenant.
- In James, He is the one who heals the sick.
- In 1 and 2 Peter, He is our Shepherd.
- In John and Jude, He is the lover coming for His bride.
- In Revelation, Jesus is King of Kings and Lord of Lords.

We can even express examples of the person of Jesus several times over in each letter of our own English alphabet.

A: Jesus is our **A**dvocate (1 John 2:1).
B: Jesus is our **B**lessed Hope (Titus 2:13).
C: Jesus is our **C**ounselor (Isaiah 9:6).
D: Jesus is our **D**eliverer (Psalms 40:17).
E: Jesus is our **E**ternal Life (Deuteronomy 33:27).
F: Jesus is our **F**ortress. (Psalm 18:2).
G: Jesus is our **G**ift from God (John 4:10).
H: Jesus is our **H**orn of salvation (Luke 1:69).
I: Jesus is our **I**ntercessor (Isaiah 53:12 and Romans 8:27).

J: Jesus is our **J**udge (Genesis 18:25 and Acts 10:42).
K: Jesus is our **K**eeper (Psalm 121:5).
L: Jesus is our **L**ight (John 1:7).
M: Jesus is our **M**ediator (1Timothy 2:5).
N: Jesus is the **N**ame above all other names (Philipians2:9).
O: Jesus is the **O**nly begotten son (John 3:16).
P: Jesus is the great **P**hysician (Luke 4:23).
Q: Jesus is our **Q**uickening spirit (1 Corinthians 15:45).
R: Jesus is our **R**efuge from the storm (Psalm 46:1).
S: Jesus is our **S**ong (Isaiah 12:2).
T: Jesus is the **T**ruth (John 14:6).
U: Jesus is our **U**nspeakable gift (2 Corinthians 9:15).
V: Jesus is our **V**ictory (1 Corinthians 15:54).
W: Jesus is our **W**itness of God (1 John 5:9).
X: Jesus is our **Ex**ceeding great reward (Genesis 15:1).
Y: Jesus is our **Y**es and amen (2 Corinthians 1:20).
Z: Jesus is our **Z**eal (John 2:17).

There are surely other alphabetical expressions, biblical examples and metaphors that typify Jesus. These are but a few, and they have been chosen by this author. But whether Jesus is presented in each book of the Bible or is expressed in each letter of the alphabet, the true nature of God is clearly shown throughout the entire Bible.

As the Bible expresses the nature of God (and Jesus) from the creation to salvation, it, of course, helps mankind to better understand the ways in which to live and glorify their Creator. The "iconic analogy" of this is depicted through the development of man, through the establishment of the Hebrews and Israelite nation.

To be sure, these iconic images and story lines of the Bible unfold and depict and describe the person of God, including Jesus Christ. But they also serve to give meaning to life itself and to bring together the Creator and His creation. There are no other texts that can collectively and in unity bring together the personalities, stories, and meanings as does the Old Testament. It is the beginning testimony and message from God. It was written over a thousand-year period in the original

Hebrew language. The fact that its content is uniform and consistent is remarkable. The following is but a brief summary of the message of the books of the Bible:

Genesis (the beginning): The first book of the Bible was written by Moses. It is the history of mankind from the creation and establishment of sin and redemption through Abraham, Isaac, and Jacob. It establishes the lineage of the Hebrews (Israelites) and other peoples of the world.

Exodus (to exit): This book was written by Moses and gives us the concepts of physical rules for an orderly life. As such, however, it gives us an understanding that it is physically impossible for physical man to obey and follow every rule, thus indicating the need for salvation. It gives us the concept of bondage to sin (Egypt) and the power of God to conquer.

Leviticus, Numbers, and Deuteronomy: These final three books written by Moses continue the history of the Hebrews and gives instructional sources of procedures for living. There are more than eighty references to Deuteronomy in the New Testament.

Joshua: This book was written partially by Joshua and/or Othniel. It, too, continues the early history of Israel, as our examples in living (for God's glory). It illustrates that civilized life is impossible when every man has "his own way." Israel did not follow laws and had considerable issues and problems.

Judges: A specific author is not known. In Israel's early and weak history, God raises characters who were either physically weak or spiritually weak, but He was still able to use them to confound the strong.

Ruth: The exact date and authorship is not known. It is an incomparable love story as Boaz marries Ruth, literally becoming an ancestor to Jesus but symbolizing the great love God has for His creation. This is the story of redemption.

Samuel 1–2, Kings 1–2, and Chronicles 1–2: The exact date and authorship of these books are not exactly known, as the writings of these texts cove a considerable time frame. It gives us an early and middle history of Israel, kings Saul, David, and Solomon (and others). The issues and lives of men and actions of Israel as a nation serve as examples of what God's Word says. It illustrates the testimony of Israel's history in which they praised God but also strayed from God. But in His faithfulness, God never forsook them and served as a background for the ministry of Jesus, which was to come later. God rules in the lives of men and nations. He judges and blesses.

Ezra: It is believed that Ezra himself wrote the book, but there is evidence that others may have contributed. It illustrates a faithful observance to the detail of the law. It demonstrates God's people called together in solemn assembly for the renewal of the covenant and gives us a priestly history of Israel.

Nehemiah: This book was probably written by Nehemiah. It describes the rebuilding of the walls of Jerusalem. It illustrates fidelity to the law and the sovereignty of God, and it gives encouragement to those who are apart from God.

Esther: The specific author is unknown. It shows that God controls all things, including His people, who may be in a distant land and may be in danger. God's people are in His hands. Though Satan is our Enemy and seeks to destroy us, wherever we are, God can save us from destruction.

Job: The exact date and authorship of Job is uncertain. It could have even been penned during the time of Solomon's reign of Israel. It wrestles with the question of suffering and evil. Although we as physical beings may have very real problems and issues of life, God knows this, and He is still in control. It is a story of unreserved living and consecration to the Lord.

Psalms: David can be ascribed to have written most of the psalms. However, Asaph, the "Sons of Korah," Solomon, and even Moses authored the rest. Psalms contain utterances from the heart concerning wisdom, love, and hopelessness. The book of Psalms illustrates the testimony of Israel's history. The book praised God, but it also did bad things. Although at times God was disappointed, He never forsook them. The book of Psalms is quoted more in the New Testament than any other Old Testament book and serves as a background for the ministry of Christ. In addition, the book of Psalms has served as an indispensable source of inspiration and devotional material.

Proverbs: Although some claim that Solomon is the author, there is also evidence that there could be/were others. This book conveys wisdom of moral quality. There is true wisdom as presented by God, and there is human wisdom. Proverbs adds to the mental insight that moral goodness and decency alone makes intelligence worthwhile.

Ecclesiastes: Although many assume that Solomon is the author and although Solomon is the central figure in the book, the exact date and authorship is unclear. It illustrates that all earthly goals when pursued as ends in themselves lead to emptiness. Life apart from God is vanity.

Song of Solomon: It is believed that Solomon wrote this book. It extols human love and godly love.

Isaiah: This book was authored by Isaiah. Although all have sinned and can be condemned, there will be those who believe and "are saved." This idea is manifest with the nation of Israel. God has a remnant and a grand and glorious future for it, which will include Judah, the messianic nation to the world.

Jeremiah: This book was authored by Jeremiah. Although there is a remnant (to be saved), there will be judgment and destruction and doom. Jerusalem ultimately falls.

Lamentation: Jeremiah is most likely the author of this book. It is the death wail of Jerusalem. It illustrates the sadness resulting from sin and its consequences.

Ezekiel: Ezekiel is the most logical author of this book. It tells of the initial fall of Judah (as in initial fall of man) but also captures the restoration and glorious future (salvation and ultimate ending for God's remnant). It gives a vision of restoration of Israel and the coming of the new era.

Daniel: Daniel is the author. It tells of the fall of Judah and a remnant that will return. It gives a vision of Israel through the centuries and describes the ultimate destruction of its enemy in end times. Although we may live in the present, God is in ultimate control of all times.

Hosea: Hosea is the author of this book. It tells of mankind's unfaithfulness and God's faithfulness. It tells of a relationship that was broken and the reasons for the breakup. God is faithful to even an unfaithful nation.

Joel: The author is Joel. It describes a vision of the gospel age, the church, and the ultimate return of Jesus Christ.

Amos: The author is Amos. Although it may seem that evil seems to triumph and reign, God's house will yet rule.

Obadiah: Obadiah is most likely the author. It describes the fall of Edom, descendants of Esau, who allied with Babylon against Israel (God's chosen people). God is universal in His power and judgment. Edom allied with Babylon against Judah and was sentenced to destruction.

Jonah: The author is Jonah. He went to preach to Nineveh (the Assyrians). It tells of God's amazing love and His interest in *all* people. It also shows that God uses the nation of Israel to proclaim His Word.

Micah: The author is Micah. It illustrates that religious rituals have no meaning to God. The only true religion is to walk justly, have mercy, and walk humbly with God.

Nahum: The author is Nahum. It tells of the doom of Nineveh (Assyria), who had destroyed the northern kingdom of Israel. Although Satan has destroyed mankind, even he will ultimately be doomed.

Habakkuk: The author is Habakkuk. Although there is currently pain, heartache, and gloom, there is the ultimate triumph for God's people through faith. It is faith that reveals that God alone is enough.

Zephaniah: The author is Zephaniah. In its description of "the day of the Lord" and the scope of His judgment because of sin, there is still redemption and ultimate supremacy of Israel (Judah). A new revelation is coming.

Haggai: The author is Haggai. So as the temple was originally built (and destroyed), a second, greater temple is coming. Though there was a temple built ... and destroyed because of sin, a new era is coming, one where there will be no sin.

Zechariah: The author is Zechariah. In the providence of God, the temple of the human heart is the abiding place of God's Spirit. The message is that we must intentionally work on the temple. In this rebuilding of the temple, the book illustrates the coming king, His house, and kingdom.

Malachi: Malachi is the author. It is a closing message of a Messianic nation.

There was a period of approximately four hundred years after the completion of the Old Testament and the writings of the New Testament. The events and history that developed during this time frame helped to reference and provide a backdrop to the developments described in the New Testament. The timing was perfect. With the text of the Old Testament and now the establishment of the New Testament, the relationship between the two accounts can give full meaning to God's Word. Again, no other text can boast of this.

Since the Old Testament describes the coming of Jesus, His life and purpose including His physical life, physical death and resurrection, certain factors of history had to develop and play out before these events of Jesus could take place. First, the "office" or positions of the Pharisees (separated one) and Sadducees began almost two centuries before the birth of Christ. As the Pharisees observed Mosaic Laws with "ceremonial purity", it was their behavior that Jesus addressed during His life that clearly had an effect on the mission of Jesus and His disciples.

However, probably one of the greatest of historical events that affected Scripture writing, including the accounts of the birth, death and resurrection of Jesus was the beginning of the Roman Empire. History records indicate that following the assassination of Julius Caesar, a power struggle ensued. Principle conspirators Marcus Brutus and Gaius Cassius took control of eastern provinces of the Roman Empire. However, forces lead by Gaius Octavius and Marc Antony defeated them in the battle of Phillipi, Macedonia. Marc Antony formed an alliance with Cleopatra and was ultimately defeated by Octavius. Octavius would change his name to Caesar Augustus (Caesar meaning deification and Augustus meaning revered or sacred) and would be named by the Roman Senate as Emperor of Rome. And it would be Caersar Augustus that would be the Roman Emperor at the time of Jesus' birth.

Meanwhile, Herod Agrippa, who initially supported Marc Antony and had ironically been named "King of the Jews", eventually found favor with Caesar Augustus. Herod had initiated an ambitious building campaign, including renovations of the Jewish (Solomon's) Temple. And it would be Herod who the wise men would ask, "Where is He that is born King of the Jews." (Matthew 2:2.) His great-grand-son Agrippa II would be the one Paul would witness to, only to be told by him, "Almost you persuade me to be a Christian" (Acts 26:28).

Included in the history between the Old and New Testaments is the development of the Herodians and Zealots which developed at opposite ends of the political spectrum. The Herodians supported Herod's (family) in just trying to maintain civil order, whereas the Zealots were patriots who opposed Rome at any cost. Judas, who betrayed Jesus, is believed to have been of this political sect.

Thus, the marking of the exact time in which the New Testament was written, telling of the birth, life, death, and resurrection of Jesus and the establishment of faithful believers and the doctrines of that faith that followed is unmatched. No other spiritual writings can equal even the timing in which it was written.

Matthew: Matthew is the author. It tells of the gospel of Christ Jesus as king. It alludes to more than a hundred Old Testament passages and confirms that Jesus is Lord.

Mark: Although there is some uncertainty, people generally believe that Mark is the author. It portrays Jesus as the "Son of God," emphasizing that Jesus is God's Son and thus is fully God. For example, at the crucifixion, we find the Roman centurion who states, "Truly, this is the son of God."

Luke: Luke is the author. It portrays Jesus as the "Son of Man," emphasizing that Jesus was fully man, thus highlighting His humanity and compassionate feelings. It is here where we find the story of the lost sheep, lost son, and the Good Samaritan.

John: Although the author is not specifically named in the book, it is accepted that John, one of the twelve disciples of Jesus and the son of Zebedee, is the author. It portrays Jesus as God. It is here where we find the great "I am" statements of Jesus. It reinforces the statement made by God to Moses at the burning bush, where God said, "I am."

Acts: The author is Luke. It tells of the spread of the gospels and the rejection of Christ by the Jews and acceptance by the Gentiles, as well as the acceptance and treatment of the early Christians.

Romans: This letter was written by Paul to the church at Rome. It is a letter of instruction and basic Christian philosophy, and it outlines the importance of righteousness and man's relationship with God through Christ. It expounds upon the laws of God in the Old Testament writings and their meanings in today's Christian world.

Corinthians 1–2: These are letters written by Paul to the church at Corinth. It gives council concerning a variety of church issues, including expression of Christians' love and concern, and it establishes Paul's authority, making credible his letters.

Galatians: This is a letter written by Paul to the churches in Galatia. This letter explains the differences and the relationship between Jewish Christian living and Gentile Christian living. It gives the message of grace that calls for faith and not that of the law that requires perfection (which we cannot achieve).

Ephesians: This letter was written by Paul to the church at Ephesus. It gives a panoramic view of God's redemptive purpose. The breadth of the entire biblical message can be seen within this letter.

Philippians: This is a letter written by Paul to the church at Philippi. It is a letter of commendation and exhortation to the local church.

Colossians: This is a letter written by Paul to the church at Colosse. It is a letter of doctrinal message to the church, reminding the church that Christ is the head of the church.

Thessalonians 1–2: These letters were written by Paul to the church at Thessalonica. These letters give us a glimpse of the early church, in which there were no specific instructions or organization. In addition, it gives sequences of events leading up to the second coming of Christ, including the Antichrist.

Timothy 1–2: These letters were written to Timothy. It is a letter of praise and exhortation and a charge to the faithful.

Titus: This is a letter written to Titus. It is a letter describing a connection between faithful men, godliness, and good works.

Philemon: This is a letter written by Paul to Philemon. It is a letter concerning principles governing relationships among Christian brothers. As Christians, there is a new frame of reference from which to learn and live.

Hebrews: The authorship of this book is uncertain. Although many support the supposition that it was authored by Paul, a great deal of evidence suggests otherwise. This letter emphasizes that only Christ could have saved us (from our sins) and only He (Jesus) can guarantee believers an entrance to the very presence of a Holy God.

James: This book was believed to be authored by James, the half brother of Jesus. It is a letter calling for vital Christianity, hearing *and* doing the Word of God.

Peter 1–2: It is well believed that Peter, a disciple of Jesus, is the author. These letters remind us that believers need to be reminded that they were once lost and not part of God's family but that they are now. There is also a call that there are indeed false prophets that wish to confound and confuse.

John 1–3: These letters were written by John, the same John who wrote the gospel of John, the disciple of Jesus. These are letters of instruction to believers, contrasting love and fellowship with that of deceit and heresy.

Jude: Jude, another half brother of Jesus, is thought to be author of this letter. It is a letter of warning against false teaching, including Gnosticism.

Revelation: The author of this book is John, the same writer of the gospel of John and of 1, 2, and 3 John. It is a revelation describing the judgment, destruction of evil, the ending of time/space (as we know it), and the beginning of a "new heaven and new earth."

From the beginning book of Genesis to the ending book of the Revelation, God's nature of Creator to Redeemer is presented with clarity and peculiar oneness. From the establishment of the Israelites and the laws to the redemption by God (Jesus) to the ending book of Revelation and the end of all time, the unity of these descriptions, accounts, and iconic illustrations is unmatched. No other literary text of any type can equal the unity and harmony of the Bible in describing God, His nature, and His attributes. The books of Bible from the Old Testament through the New Testament are in complete harmony and truly fitly framed together.

7. There Was a Beginning, and There Will Be an End.

It is true that most major religions teach that there was a creation and there will be an end. However, the Bible goes deeper. The Bible teaches that there is good and evil. However, that is the purpose of Jesus—to ultimately conquer evil.

"The beginning" illustrates that God existed even before the beginning our physical time. "In the beginning God created the heaven and the earth" (Genesis 1:1). "In the beginning was the Word, and the Word was with God and the Word was God. The same was in the beginning with God" (John 1:1–2).

The duration of this physical time and space is in control by God. He created it.

> I will open rivers in high places, and fountains in the midst of the valleys: I will make the wilderness a pool of water, and the dry land springs of water. I will plant in the wilderness the cedar, the shittah tree, and the myrtle, and the oil tree; I will

> set in the desert the fir tree, and the pine tree, and the box tree together: that they may see, and know, and consider, and understand together, that the hand of the Lord has done this, and the Holy One of Israel has created it. (Isaiah 41:18–20)

God challenged Job to understanding His (God's) works and wisdom. "Where were you when I laid the foundations of the earth? Declare if you have understanding" (Job 38:4). God continues, "Do you know the laws of heaven? Can you set the dominion thereof in the earth? Can you (Job) lift up your voice to the clouds, that the abundance of waters may cover you? Can you send lightning?" (Job 38:33–5).

However, in order to validate that God will indeed conquer evil, there must come an end to this physical world as we know it. But there will also be an everlasting time afterward. As before time, God was in His holy realm. Within the framework of good and evil and holy and righteous, God will have redeemed His creation and thus returned to man (having been able to conquer the evil) an everlasting, holy, and pure family of God.

> I saw a great white throne, and him that sat on it, from whose face, the earth and heaven fled away; and there was found no place for them. And I saw the dead, small and great, stand before God; and the books were opened: and another book was opened, which is the book of life: and the dead were judged out of those things which were written in the books, according to their works. And the sea gave up its dead which were in it; and death and hell delivered up the dead which were in them: according to their works. And death and hell were cast into the lake of fire. This is the second death. And whosoever was not found written in the book of life was cast into the lake of fire. (Revelation 20:11–15)

Now consider the following two passages: "And I saw a new heaven and a new earth: for the first heaven and the first earth were passed away; and there was no more sea" (Revelation 21:1). "And he said unto me, It is done, I am the alpha and Omega, the beginning and the end" (Revelation 21:6).

The Bible begins with the beginning of all things and ends with the ending of all things. As one ponders the general text of the Bible from its beginning to its end, the person can see that it certainly describes the nature of God, the power and judgment of sin, and the redemption by Jesus, as well as guidelines to a meaningful relationship between God and man ... and between man and man. The exact wording as penned in Scripture as well as the iconic, visual, and real examples illustrated in the Bible indicate that man could not have simply written the content of the Bible but that God made it fitly framed together Himself.

CHAPTER 2

How Our Bible Came to Be

The Significance of the History of the Bible

A major thread that holds together the fabric of Scripture is how such a text written by so many over such a long period of time could even come together at all! At the time of their writings, the books that now make up the Bible were certainly recognized by contemporary Hebrews as inspired by God. Jewish scribes and priests were given the task of maintaining and recopying text for future generations. Other Jewish writings appeared, but these were never seriously considered as inspired.

By the time of Christ, this collection of Scripture was known as "the Law and the Prophets," and as previously noted; Jesus exclaimed and quoted these Scripture verses. In fact, He even accused many of the scribes and Pharisees, the so-called experts in Scripture of that time, of not knowing the Scripture. "You do err, not knowing the scriptures nor the power of God" (Matthew 22:29).

The first five books of the Bible, specifically Genesis, Exodus, Leviticus, Numbers, and Deuteronomy, are called the Pentateuch. They were written by Moses. The rest of the books of the Old

Testament were written by judges, kings, prophets, and others. Even after hundreds of years, these scriptures were well known among the people.

Shortly after the death and resurrection of Jesus, many began to write accounts of the life of Christ, followed by letters or epistles, as well as other writings describing Christian living and tying together Old Testament philosophies of God, holiness, grace, mercy, the plan of salvation, and the ending of physical time. By the end of the first century, all Scripture had been completed.

Certainly, the writings of Moses, the prophets, and others were esteemed as inspired by God and considered Holy Scripture. However, other Jewish writings from between the testaments, such as the Macabees, Tobit, Judith, and others, were sometimes read in synagogues and early churches. Although considered spiritually helpful, many church officials objected to their use, fearing that they would be confused with the Scriptures because they were not written by prophets or apostles. Thus, many asked the question: What is actually Scripture, and what is not?"

The fact that the original Scripture itself was written by more than forty different authors over a time frame of 1,500 years is remarkable in itself. But the subsequent gathering and collection of these texts is also remarkable. Unlike a text written by an individual and then possibly rewritten, translated, and handed down from generation, the collection of texts we now call the Bible was handed down and translated in such a way that the original communication from God is still intact today. God's message to man has not altered through the eons of years.

But there are those who may wonder as to how the Bible of today came together in the first place. The theme of the Bible is so multifaceted, covers such a long period of time, and was written by so many people of different backgrounds that it is difficult to understand how it could come together at all. How was it fitly framed together?

The Bible certainly is about God, but the nature of God is enormous and comprehensive. It includes the power of God, the righteousness of God, the mercy of God, and the judgment of God just to name a few. Conveying these immense tenets of Scripture is a huge undertaking.

The Bible says that God created the heavens and the earth. But God did not only create the spiritual. He also created the physical. This is enormous because He created the laws of chemistry and physics, including all the "laws of nature." And each aspect of the physical depends on another for existence and substance.

The original language of the Old Testament written by Moses and other Old Testament authors was Hebrew, although parts of Daniel, Ezra and Jeremiah were written in Aramaic. Thus, as cultures came and developed, as did their languages, it is amazing that the original language of Hebrew remained constant from the writing of Moses around 1400 BC to the writing of Malachi about 400 BC. The Old Testament could be divided into three categories—historical, poetical, and prophetical. All of these books of Scripture were written and passed down from generation to generation.

However, Greek culture, business, and language became increasingly used after 400 BC. Following the ascension of Alexander the Great to the throne of Greece around 330 BC, the Greek culture had spread throughout the known world. Thus, the Greek language was the language of politics, business, and education. Before long, most Hebrews had even lost the ability to read and write in the Hebrew language.

Old Testament Scripture was still read in Hebrew by rabbis and used in synagogue worship, but eventually, the books had to be translated into the Greek language. According to tradition, around 200 BC, seventy-two Jewish elders assembled in Alexandria to translate the five books of Moses (the Pentateuch) into the Greek language. This translation was supposed to have taken seventy-two days to complete, but the entire Old Testament was soon translated into the Greek language. This translation is known as the Septuagint. (*Septuaginta* is Latin for "seventy.")

Although the scrolls that comprised the Hebrew Bible were probably the Scriptures that were used during the time of Jesus, it is likely that Greek-speaking Jews used the Septuagint as well. For example, many believe that when Stephen was accused (Acts 6) and stoned to death, those that debated and discussed his actions probably used the Septuagint for reference (although they selectively misused these Scriptures). Paul could have very well used the Septuagint as he delivered his message throughout Asia Minor. At the time, there were certainly many languages being used and Latin was the language of the Roman Empire. However, it is interesting that the unity of New Testament text (beginning with Matthew about 50 AD until the book of Revelation written by John around 90 AD was written mostly in the Greek language.

The New Testament books began to appear: Matthew, James, John in Palestine, followed by letters from Paul, such Galatians, Ephesians, Colossians, and others in Greece. Titus was written in Crete. Mark, Acts, and Romans were written from Rome. Other books followed, and they were read throughout the Mediterranean. It is interesting to note that though the Old Testament was read in a relatively confined geographic region, the New Testament was read throughout a wider area. Paul quoted as Scripture in 1 Timothy 5:18, "The Laborer is worthy of his hire." This passage is found in Matthew 10:10 and Luke 10:7. This mention would seem to show evidence that Matthew and Luke were in existence and were regarded as Scripture.

Historical issues made the writing, the collecting, and the handing down of early Christian writing difficult. There was no such thing as printing, and copying was arduous at best. The early Christians were persecuted by Rome as well as other cultural societies. In addition, there were other writings that were both good and fraudulent. Some grouped these writings as Scripture. There were no organizational churches and no councils or conferences where people could meet and compare notes. Thus, the earliest collection of New Testament books varied, and unanimity as to which books belonged to the New Testament was slow.

It would become apparent that both the Old Testament and New Testaments writings would need to be collected and recorded. Because of early Roman influence, Latin translation of the Old Testament seemed natural. However, early Latin translations were taken from the Greek Septuagint and not from the original Hebrew. Thus, even early on, questions began to arise regarding the quality of the translation. In addition, what was actually Scripture, and what was not? Thus, as translators needed to convey the exact message of the Scripture, it was indeed necessary to examine and scrutinize each noun and verb to ensure proper translation and intent of the original author. And this was accomplished.

One of the earliest writers to provide a list of the Old Testament books was Melito of Sardis. Around 170 AD, he listed all the books of our Old Testament except the book of Esther. He was the first known writer to refer to this collection of books as "the books of the old covenant" (or Old Testament). When Constantine became Roman Emperor in 306 AD, he made Eusebius his religious advisor. Under orders from the emperor, Eusebius conducted research to determine the general consensus about which books they should include in the New Testament. The twenty-seven books of the New Testament we have today were the exact same ones he included. By the late 300s, it was clear that these twenty-seven New Testament books were considered Scripture.

In 363, the Council of Laodicea published 60 cannons or rules for the guidance of the church (Roman Catholic Church). It determined what would and would not be included in the Bible or read at church. It listed the books of the Old Testament (including Esther) and the twenty-seven books of New Testaments. By 405 AD, Jerome, a great Bible scholar of the time, completed his translation of the Old Testament into Latin directly from the original Hebrew language. It included twenty-two books, which later corresponded to the thirty-nine books of the modern Old Testament. Books that were included in the list of the Old Testament and New Testaments became known as the Cannon (or canonical books). Books that were not included or viewed as not Scripture were known as the Apocrypha. Some of the Apocrypha included Baruch, Letter of Jeremiah (not to be confused with the book of Jeremiah), Judith, Tobit, Wisdom, the Ecclesianticus (not to be confused with Ecclesiastes), and the two books of the Maccabees.

In the times following Jerome's translation, further questions and attacks on the validity and quality of Scripture came to the forefront. Jerome's version of the Bible was known as the Latin Vulgate because it was written in the vulgar or common form of Latin (language of the people). However, certain church leaders wanted particular Apocryphal books included in the Cannon. Authority of Scripture soon fell to the authority of the Roman Catholic Church, specifically to the Pope. Riddled with scandal, the early Roman Catholic Church developed ecclesiastical dogmas, including beliefs in purgatory, the practice of masses for the dead, and praying for the dead to save them from their sins. This practice can be found in the writings of the Maccabees, which are considered Apocrypha. However, these writings are not in concert with Scripture, regarding redemption and God's plan of salvation, thus the separation from the Cannon into the Apocrypha. Then again, this is why some wanted many of the Apocrypha included as Scripture.

By the fourteenth and fifteenth centuries, the English language became the universal language of record. The need for an English translation of the Bible was now apparent. John Wycliffe stirred up interest to produce a translation of the Bible in the language of the common people. He published the Wycliffe Version around 1400, though it is not certain how much of it he himself translated. But this Bible was most popular, and it was the first complete Bible to appear in England.

However, the political climate and atmosphere of the world began to change. In 1453, Constantinople, the capital of the Eastern Roman Empire, fell. Eastern and Western Europe struggled as new political powers emerged. Yet the Roman Catholic Church strove to maintain religious power. By 1455, Gutenberg had invented the movable type printing press, making possible easy and accurate copies of reading material. Universal literacy and education was now possible.

As more individuals were able to read and study Scripture, more discovered the unity of some "scriptural text" and the non-unity of other "scriptural text". Many began to debate whether the Apocryphal books should be included within the Cannon. In 1517, Martin Luther nailed his ninety-five theses to the church door at Wittenberg, questioning the doctrines of the Roman Catholic Church, and the Protestant Reformation had begun. In 1534, Luther published his German translation of the Bible. With respect to the Apocrypha, Luther held that "what preaches Christ" should be dominant in Scripture. And because the Apocryphal books did not stay that course, they should not be included as Scripture, according to Luther. In 1526, he printed the New Testament translated in German.

In 1546 at the Council of Trent, the Roman Catholic Church answered the attacks of the Protestants regarding the Apocryphal books. In essence, the Catholic Church rejected Jerome's Latin Vulgate Bible, which had separated the Apocrypha from the Cannon. In effect this meant that, at least within the Roman Catholic faith, the Apocrypha was to be kept as part of the Bible. However, today, many Roman Catholic scholars do recognize a difference between these two groups of books, even if the church officially does not.

As time passed, the languages of the people subtly changed, especially the English language. William Tyndale, an Oxford- and Cambridge-trained scholar, published an English version of the New Testament in 1526. His desire was to produce a new edition of the Bible in the English of his day, one translated from the original Hebrew and Greek. But the Bishop of London would not permit its introduction, so Tyndale resorted to smuggling. He was eventually kidnapped, tried as a heretic, and burned at the stake in 1536. As discourse between the Roman Catholic Church and the monarchy of England escalated coupled with the invention of the printing press and the explosion of the Protestant Reformation, English translations of the Bible became increasingly in demand.

King Henry VIII, who had separated from the Roman Catholic Church in 1533, authorized an English translation of the Bible. However, just before the death of Tyndale, there appeared the first complete Bible printed in the English tongue. It was the Cloverdale Bible. Miles Cloverdale had been commissioned by Thomas Cromwell, King Henry VIII's secretary of state, to translate the entire Bible into the English language. His Bible was based on the Latin Vulgate, Tyndale's version, and the German Bible of Martin Luther. He was the first to completely separate the Apocrypha from the Old Testament and place it as an appendix, placing those books after Malachi. Subsequent English translations soon followed.

Cloverdale played a major role in the development of the next English Bible. And when it was printed in 1538, it measured nine inches by fifteen inches (the print was 8 1/2 x 13 inches). Thus, it was called "the Great Bible" because of its large size, and every parish church in England was supposed to use this version[1]. This Bible had Cloverdale's introduction to the Apocrypha, but it called these writings Hagiographa, meaning holy writings.

The religious climate of England changed again, however, when Mary I became queen in 1553. Because she was Catholic, reformers and biblical translators were singled out. John Rogers and Thomas Cranmer, archbishop of Canterbury, were both burned at the stake. Copies of the Great Bible were removed from churches, and public reading from them was banned. During this turmoil, many English church leaders fled to Geneva, Switzerland. There, a group of scholars produced an English version called the Geneva Bible. It is considered the most accurate version up to the Authorized King James Version.

Printed in 1560 and again in 1652, it was the first English version to use numbered verses as separate paragraphs. (Robert Estienne is credited for developing the chapter-verse division of his Greek New Testament Bible.) The Geneva Bible was the Bible used by Shakespeare, and it was the Bible that brought over to the New World on the *Mayflower.* Used by the Puritans, this version of the Bible certainly initiated the Christian foundation laid for the United States. During the reign of Elizabeth (1558–1603), the Geneva Bible was most used in homes while the Great Bible was the choice for use in church services. The Geneva Bible continued the practice of placing the Apocrypha at the end of the Old Testament. However, some did not approve of the Apocrypha, and in 1599, an edition was printed without the Apocrypha.

Following the accession of Queen Elizabeth in 1558 and the popularity of the Geneva Bible, Anglican Church authorities decided to produce a Bible that could bear the authority of the Church of England. This Bible became known as the Bishops' Bible, first published in 1568. The Great Bible as well as Hebrew and Greek text were used to develop this translation. Subsequently, there are fewer differences between the Bishops' Bible and the King James Version than any other preceding version. Meanwhile, an English translation of the Bible produced for Catholics was the Rheims-Douay Bible, which was published in 1609. It was translated from the Latin Vulgate, not the original Hebrew and Greek.

Confusion still existed as a result of the use of these separate translations. Story has it that as King James was on his way to London to receive his crown he was presented with a petition by Puritan clergy to help resolve the differences in these variations of Scripture. He subsequently called for a conference of Anglican bishops and Puritan clergy. During the conference, known as the Hampton Court Conference, a motion was made to create a new English version of Scripture. Because previous versions existed and were being used, the motion was voted down. However, it appealed to the king.

Fifty-four of the greatest biblical scholars in Great Britain were assembled to take on this task. The new translation was to be taken from the original Hebrew and Greek. Work began in 1607, and in 1610, they completed the project with publication of the first edition of the Authorized Version, sometimes referred to as the King James Version of the Bible. Eventual studies concerning the King James Version reveal that about 80 percent of the text is actually taken from the Tyndale Bible. It included the Apocrypha. However, by 1626, copies were being produced that did not contain the Apocrypha.

For more than three hundred years, this English translation has been the standard from which the Scripture or Word of God has been studied. In 1782, Robert Aitken printed the first King James Bibles in America. In 1833, after he produced his own famous dictionary, Noah Webster printed his own version of the King James Bible.

Attempts had been made to develop a single revised version (American and English) of the King James Bible. In 1901, the Revised American Standard Bible was published. In 1971, the New American Standard Bible was published. It took eleven years to complete, and it was translated by an editorial board of fifty-four Greek and Hebrew scholars. In 2002, the English Standard Version was published.

Certainly, as dialogues and word usage of English has changed, there have been other English translations. Overall, at least one of the two testaments has been translated into 2,479 languages and dialects, and the full Protestant Bible has been translated into 451 languages. Various portions of the Bible have been translated in more than four thousand different languages and dialects, far more than any other manuscript. More than one billion Bibles have been printed, by far the most printed book ever! What other text can boast of such a storied history?

George Washington has been quoted as saying, “It is impossible to rightly govern the world without God and the Bible.” Abraham Lincoln said, “I believe the Bible is the best gift God has given to man. All the good from the Savior of the world is communicated through this book.” Even Isaac Newton, the great science scholar of Great Britain, has been quoted as saying of the Bible, “There are more sure marks of authenticity in the Bible than any profane history that was stated[2, 3].”

Without a doubt, Satan has made every attempt to discredit and destroy this message from God. From the original writings of more than forty different authors over 1,600 years to the subsequent collection and printing of the texts we now view, no other book has traversed the path and emerged unscathed as the Bible. No other book in human existence has been written, translated, retranslated, paraphrased, and published more and in more languages than the Bible. The web that put it together in the beginning and the web that holds it together today is one web. It is the tapestry of God that fully reveals that the Bible is truly fitly framed together. What other writing has such a history?

Summary of the History of the Bible

1400 BC: Moses wrote the first five books of the Bible.

400 BC: Malachi writes the last of the Old Testament books.

200 BC: Completion of the Septuagint (Greek manuscript).

95 AD: The epistle John writes the book of Revelation, the last of the New Testament books, completing the Scripture.

300 AD: The twenty-seven books of the New Testament are recognized as the Cannon of the Scripture.

382 AD: Jerome's Latin Vulgate is produced, containing thirty-nine Old Testament books, fourteen Apocrypha, and twenty-seven New Testament books.

500 AD: Various parts of Scripture had been translated in more than five hundred languages.

600 AD: The Catholic Church forbids the reading of the Bible in any language other than Latin.

1384 AD: John Wycliff produces a handwritten English manuscript of the entire Bible.

1455 AD: Gutenberg invents the printing press. The first book printed is Gutenberg's Bible in Latin.

1516 AD: Erasmus produces a Greek-Latin parallel of the New Testament.

1522 AD: Martin Luther produces a German version of the New Testament.

1526 AD: William Tyndale produces the first New Testament printed in English.

1535 AD: Myles Cloverdale produces the first complete Bible printed in English, one based on the old Latin Vulgate.

1539 AD: The Great Bible was published.

1560 AD: The Geneva Bible is published.

1568 AD: The Bishops' Bible is published.

1611 AD: The Kings James Bible is printed.

1782 AD: Robert Aitken's Bible is the first English Bible printed in America.

1833 AD: Noah Webster's Bible is printed.

1901 AD: The American Standard Version Bible is published.

1971 AD: The New American Standard Bible is published.

2002 AD: The English Standard Version is published.

REFERENCES

1. English Bible History. http://www.greatsite.com/timeline-english-bible-history/(Retrieved April 30, 2013)

2. Why Do We Believe the Bible Is the Word Of God? The Fourth Reason. http://www.arabicbible.com/formuslims/questionsanswers/1555-why-we-believe-the-bible-is-the-word-of-god.html?start-4. (Retrieved April 30, 2013)

3. The Bible-Quotes From Famous Men. http:/www.why-the-bible-com/bible.htm. (Retrieved April 30, 2013).

[Note. There are many internet sites that cite quotations from others. And some of these quotes are questioned by current groups for various reasons and intents.]

CHAPTER 3

Numbers in the Bible

The Spiritual Significance of Numbers in the Bible

The act of counting and custom of numbers has long been intricate elements of the culture of mankind. As far back as Neolithic times, counting was widespread. The use of numbers date back to the ancient Mesopotamian civilizations around 5000 BC. The old kingdom of the Egyptian civilization (3000 BC) developed inscriptions and illustrations depicting numeric values. Geometry and algebra soon developed.

The Greek mathematician Pythagorea (580–500 BC) coined the word "mathematics" from the Greek *mathema,* meaning "subject of instruction." Pythagorean developed the infamous Pythagorean equation describing length and angles of triangles. His followers coined a motto, "Everything is number." Eventually, counting with numbers led to more advanced math, calculus, and differential equations. From the ancient principles of Archimedes (287–212 BC) to the current theory of relativity and quantum mechanics equations of Einstein and Hawking, math is a major communicator.

All kinds of properties and interesting structures concerning numbers have long been known. By themselves, numbers may not be important without context; however, since the ancient Mesopotamian civilization and certainly more specific in the modern era, people can develop some fascinating and intriguing scenarios by using numbers. For example, if one were to write all the numbers from one to nine in ascending order and then in a descending order, we get the following:

12,345,678,987,654,321

It turns out that this number is equal to this:

(111, 111, 111) x (111, 111, 111).

This makes a pattern of three sets of ones squared or $(111, 111, 111)^2$.

There are many other interesting mathematical structures and complex chains of numbers. Interesting chains or patterns include the following:

$$1 + 2 = 3$$
$$4 + 5 + 6 = 7 + 8$$
$$9 + 10 + 11 + 12 = 13 + 14 + 15.$$

Another interesting arrangement occurs with the number thirteen (and its reverse, thirty-one).

13 x 13 = 169

31 x 31 = 961

The development of computer language and the numbers depicting bits and bytes stem from the numbers zero (0) and one (1). In all things, an entity either "is" (1), or it "is not" (0). For example, the letter "A" either *is* or *is not* the letter "A." A shade of the color blue either *is* blue, or it *is not* blue. Thus, the descriptive language that drives computers can be simplistically illustrated by a series of zeros (0) or ones (1).

The use of numeric values has other significant meanings. For example, the words "mite," "jot," and "tittle" speak of something that is considered small and maybe of little value. However, these small things can be most important. In addition, the use of the word "pair" implies two, such as a "pair of shoes," and a gross of pencils implies twelve (a dozen) or 144 pencils. Thus, numbers may have actual values, yet when used in certain ways within the language, these can add a fuller, more enriched meaning to the conversation.

Placement of significance within numbers is very important. Take, for example, the numbers 0000001 and 0001000 and 1000000. Simple placement of the number 1 changes the numeric value of the entire sequence. So it is in the world of man. The use of numbers enhances the dialogue, yet placement of what is significant is critical to the outcome.

In fact, even the magnitude of numbers can seem meaningless. Consider the magnitudes of millions, billions, trillions, or quadrillion. Are greater magnitudes given greater priority?

- One million seconds ago was twelve days ago.
- One billion seconds ago was 1975.
- One trillion seconds ago was 29,700 BC.
- One quadrillion seconds ago was 30,800,000 years ago.

There is a story of a man who was an architect. He was a loving family man with a wife and small son. He wanted to be with his son and run beside him as his son learned to ride his bike. However, the man kept putting off being with his son because of his work. One Saturday morning, the man was at a job site instead of being at home with his son. There was an accident. His son fell into the dugout portion for the foundation of the building and became paralyzed, never to walk again. He was not concerned with his physical pain or his inability to walk again. Mentally, he anguished over having neglected his son and never being able to walk alongside him as his child rode a bike. His priority had been his work. He now wished he had had a different priority.

To be sure, there have been many decisions of man where the results of those decisions did not occur because of proper placement of priority. It would seem that not only is the God of creation a pure mathematician, but His use of language utilizing numbers is yet another piece of fabric that is woven into the Bible. In no writings of man can the lessons of numbers and priority be found like those found in the Bible. No other complete writings display the significance of an almighty God, His creation, the result of sin, His love, His grace, and His mercy, and His desire to have fellowship with man.

Since the formative years of the development of man's civilization, there have been unique relationships between letters of the alphabet (written language) and numbers. The ancient Hebrew language utilized letters (no vowels) of their alphabet to indicate numbers (1500 BC). Thus, even in the spelling of words using the Hebrew alphabet, a mathematical derivative was created. This assigning of numbers to letters of an alphabet is defined as *gematria*. For example, the spelling of David (as in King David of Israel), DVD can also be the number 14. This spelling of words and depiction of mathematics occurred around 1000 BC, yet Matthew (around 60 AD) records two major fourteen genealogy sections that followed the life of King David (Matthew 1:1–17), emphasizing the importance of numbers developed and used in Scripture. But it also shows the unity of Scripture using all that is written (Old Testament and New Testament), including gematria regardless of the time span in which it was written.

Here are some modern day examples of using gematria to the English alphabet and language. Suppose the alphabet

A B C D E F G H I J K L M N O P Q R S T U V W X Y Z

is represented as:

1 2 3 4 5 6 7 8 9 10 11 12 13 14 15 16 17 18 19 20 21 22 23 24 25 26

then:

H-A-R-D-W-O-R-K can be represented numerically as
8+1+18+4+23+15+18+11 = 98 … (or 98 percent)

K-N-O-W-L-E-D-G-E can be represented numerically as
11+14+15+23+12+5+4+7+5 = 96 … (or 96 percent)
A-T-T-I-T-U-D-E can be represented numerically as
1+20+20+9+20+21+4+5 = 100 … (or 100 percent)

L-O-V-E-O-F-G-O-D can be represented numerically as
12+15+22+5+15+6+7+15+4 = 101 … (or 101 percent)

These are interesting examples of gematria application to the English language. So we can have some fun with numbers and gematria. This is not to imply that we can or cannot have fun with numeric expressions, including gematria found within the Bible. Although gematria can be detected throughout Scripture, we do need to be careful how we attempt to create or make things seem a certain way just to elevate or magnify a particular point of view. However, we can examine the numbers embedded within the original language of the Bible and find that there are certain patterns that emerge. In addition to gematria, other examples using numbers can be seen.

Numbers expressions that are specifically mentioned in the Bible are used with great precision. In the field of science and math, accuracy can be defined as "hitting the target." Hitting a bull's-eye in a target would be what is termed "accurate". Accuracy means hitting a target exactly where you desire to hit the target. Precision, on the other hand, is being able to repeat a process. You may not hit the bull's eye (of the target), but you may consistently hit the target a little down and to the left. Thus you are hitting the target consistently in the same spot. This is precision. It is the process of repeating in a consistent manner. The Bible is consistent in its use of numbers. From Genesis to the book of Revelation, the specific numbers listed in the text are important because they are mentioned. But because their usages are also consistent, there is significant meaning to that as well. This is unique only to the Bible as it was written by so many individuals over so long a time period.

Certainly, the specific verbiage of the Hebrew, Greek, and Arabic language of the original text of the Bible depicts the image and character of God. Even the numbers and numeric values found in the Scriptures are in complete harmony with other aspects of the scripture, and these add fullness and verification to the purpose of the Holy Scripture. A student of the scriptures can develop a closer relation to God through a greater understanding of His character, and a greater understanding of God's character can be revealed through the study of numeric meanings.

This chapter is intended to present useful information regarding the biblical text and not dabble into the occultism of numerology. It is not an exhaustive study of the spiritual or symbolic meanings of numbers that are utilized in the scriptures. No amount of time, ink, and paper could fully expound upon the completeness and fullness of God. Although many aspects of Scripture may seem difficult to understand, including the use of numbers, there are no obscure fitting of the various numbers utilized in the Scriptures. On the other hand, there should not be an intentional and artificial interpretation by man as to the significance of these numbers, such as special codes or hidden messages. Numeric patterns shown are code or anything of the sort, but just simple patterns that consistently emerge through the entire Scriptures.

There have previously been numerous studies and exposes dedicated to interpretation, understanding, and meaning of various numeric values as shown in Scripture. Thematics has been defined as a Bible code, using numbers to uncover hidden meanings in Scripture. Some have attempted to expound upon numbers (those actually given in Scripture and numbers that are humanly derived) as if there are secret codes or hidden codes found in Scripture and expressed in numbers. Extreme care needs to be taken that concepts and "theology of man," including man's imagination (hidden or secret codes), is not written into the scriptures. However, God has woven a fabric of numbers throughout His Word. The Holy Scripture should be simply read and understood for what it truly is—the divinely inspired Word of God!

As with any writings, including fiction, nonfiction, poetry, etc., the author's choice of words, examples, illustrations, and archetypes is usually expressed to highlight, more fully explain, and resolve that which is being communicated. In addition to His use of the nation of

Israel to illustrate His meaning, purpose, and character, God, in His infinite wisdom and understanding, has used numbers (in addition to an alphabet language) to communicate with man.

As one studies the Scriptures, it is apparent that numbers have a spiritual significance in the Hebrew, Greek, and Arabic languages. Again, however, this is not a study in thematic or some hidden numeric code. This is a view of how certain numbers have a real significant meaning and how God uses these to more fully (and accurately) fulfill His communication with man. Thus, we can obtain a better comprehension of what God is saying through the Scriptures, drawing us closer to our God and enhancing our Christian lives. The ingenious and perpetual use of these numeric meanings throughout the Bible to add color and clarity to God's Word can only come from God. In His infinite wisdom, He gave us the Scripture "as is," and through the power of the Holy Spirit, His Word can be understood.

In mathematics, a prime number is a number that cannot be divisible evenly. Thus, the numbers 1, 3, 5, 7, 11, 13, 17, etc., are prime numbers. Though there are many other numbers that can be expounded upon, this chapter will simply summarize the significance of the numbers 1, 2, 3, 4, 5, 6, 7, 8, 9, 10, 11, 12, 13, 14, 15, 16, 17, 40, 153, and the infamous 666. Therefore, the first seven prime numbers are included. Examining these numbers should support the thesis that though the Bible was written over a period of 1,500 years by many writers, the unity of the numbers and their meanings used in Scripture augment the web of the given Word of God as fitly framed together. At the outset, a simple synopsis of these numbers and their spiritual meanings are as follows:

One (1): The number one is the first prime number. It represents *unity*, the omnipotence of God, His unity, and His never-changing character. God is and will always be. But in addition, He will always be the same. Unlike society, whose values and mores change with time, God's values, ideals, and judgments never change.

Two (2): The number two represents a *difference*, a contrast, or an alternative.

Three (3): The number three is the second prime number. It represents *divine perfection*, the fullness and completeness of a perfect God (His person, which is Father, Son and Holy Spirit, His perfect creation, and His perfect plan of salvation).

Four (4): The number four represents the *creation*, the fullness and completeness of material earth as well as the strife and hardships physical man face (north, east, south, west, and all pertaining therein).

Five (5): The number five is the third prime number. It represents *grace*. Of the traits that man has (and God-given), he is still weak (without God) and thus *needs* God's grace. Physical traits and characteristics of humans are not sufficient enough for his salvation.

Six (6): The number six represents *imperfection* (of anything), the incompleteness of man, and the physical apart from God.

Seven (7): The number seven is the fourth prime number. It represents *spiritual perfection*, the fullness and complete perfection of an omnipotent, holy, righteous God (who is *spirit*).

Eight (8): The number eight represents a *new beginning*.

Nine (9): The number nine represents *finality* (including judgment).

Ten (10): The number ten represents divine *order* or *ordinal perfection* (not to be confused with the number seven). With respect to *order*, nothing is needed. Nothing is lacking. The cycle of creation in perfection, the fall of man in imperfection, and the redemption and restoring of man through a perfect God is complete and lacks nothing. Although man failed to maintain his perfection after creation, God's provision of salvation through Jesus, His Son, is sufficient.

Eleven (11): The number eleven is the fifth prime number. It represents a *state of disorder* or *disorganized*. It signifies a state that is not perfect and *disintegrating*.

Twelve (12): The number twelve represents *governmental perfection*, the perfection of government, or organizational aspects associated with government both on earth and in heaven. The organization in which God placed man is perfect and complete both in the physical world and in the spiritual world. There is divine order in all aspects of the realm of God, including "heaven and earth." It is the divine perfection expressed in His creation (3 x 4 = 12) and the two *added* together to get spiritual perfection (3 + 4 = 7).

Thirteen (13): The number thirteen is the sixth prime number. It represents *corruption* and *rebellion*, general enemies of God.

Fourteen (14): The number fourteen represents *deliverance and salvation*. It is a double portion of spiritual perfection (7 +7 or 7 x 2 = 14).

Fifteen (15): The number fifteen represents *grace multiplied three times*. (3 x 5 = 15). It refers to the acts of God that occurred because of His nature (Father, Son, and Holy Spirit).

Sixteen (16): The number sixteen represents *God's unconditional and steadfast love for Israel ... and us.*

Seventeen (17): The number seventeen is the seventh prime number. It represents the *perfection of spiritual order*. The number just happens to be the seventh prime number in math. Within the perfection of spiritual order is the elimination of the enemies of God.

Forty (40): The number forty represents *testing and trials* ... or a period of trial and renewal.

One Hundred and Fifty-Three (153): Is a number listed only once in the Bible. It is a number divisible by three and best summarizes all other numbers.

Six Hundred and Sixty-Six (666): The number 666 is actually a number of *a name*. It represents the concentrated expression of the trinity of the perfection of humans, or rather, the perfection of imperfection. It is the exact and complete opposite of a righteous and holy God. Human pride and independence from God is in complete opposition to Jesus.

The following numbers and listed examples certainly are not a complete citing of illustrations listed in the Bible, but they are at least sample representatives that can be explained.

The Number One (1)

The number *one* in the Scripture represents absolute unity and singleness. There is only one certain painting. There is only one vacation spot. Many in an organization want to "be on the same page" in the operations. There is only one ... you. There is only one God! Thus, the number one can represent the absolute unity and singleness of God. Jesus said, "I and my father are one" (John 10:30). You may also consider the following: "That they all may be as one, as you Father are in me, that they also may be one with us: that the world may believe that you have sent me" (John 17:21). "There is one body, and one Spirit, even as you are called in one hope of your calling. One Lord, one faith, one baptism, one God and Father of all who is above all, and through all, and in you all" (Ephesians 4:4–6).

There can be no doubt as to the significance of this number. Unity can be defined as being indivisible and not made up of other numbers. It is independent of all other numbers but is the source of all others. So it is concerning the deity of God. This message is illustrated throughout the scriptures. "Hear, O Israel, the Lord your God is one Lord" (Deuteronomy 6:4). It does not deny the doctrine of the Trinity, but it excludes absolutely another Lord. Thus, it thwarts any attempt of idolatry. The first commandment given to man through Moses states, "You shall have no other gods" (Exodus 20:3). In addition, it denotes that there is only one source of salvation. "Jesus said, I am the way, the truth and the life: no man comes to the Father, but by me" (John 14:6).

The number *one* marks a beginning, which also denotes an end. "In the beginning, God—" (Genesis 1:1). "I am the alpha and omega, the beginning and the end, the first and the last" (Revelation 22:13).

Thus, there is only *one* God and *one* way to everlasting life with our Creator. Therefore, His creative plan deserves notice and is worthy of understanding. There is nothing that does not begin with God. "Seek you first the kingdom of God and His righteousness; and all these things shall be added unto you" (Matthew 6:33). "There is a way that seems right unto a man, but the end thereof are the ways of death" (Proverbs 14:12).

"God first, God only" is the great proclamation of the Scripture. Psalm 33:1–9 states,

> Rejoice in the Lord, O you righteous: for praise is comely for the upright. Praise the Lord with the Harp: sing unto him with the psaltery and an instrument of ten strings. Sing unto him a new song; play skillfully with a loud noise. For the word of the Lord is right; and all his works are done in truth. He loves righteousness and judgment; the earth is full of his goodness of the Lord. By the word of the Lord were the heavens made; and all the host of them by the breath of his mouth. He gathers the water of the sea together as a heap: he lays up the depth in storehouses. Let all the earth fear the Lord: let all the inhabitants of the world stand in awe of him. For he spoke, and it was done; he commanded, and it stood fast.

On the first Christmas the angels sang, "Glory to God in the highest" (Luke 2:14). In Revelation 19:1 (at the end of time), there is continued praise, "I heard a great voice of much people in heaven saying, Alleluia; salvation and glory and honor and power, unto the Lord our God."

Thus, the number *one* is the foundation of other numeric values, both in terms of math and symbolically speaking. Without the number one, there can be no other number. Without the one and only God, nothing can exist anyway.

- And they shall be as *one* flesh (Genesis 2:24).
- The people is *one* (Genesis 11:6). (Note the singular verb "is.")
- The Lord our God is *one* Lord (Deuteronomy 6:4, Mark 12:29).

- And call no man your father upon the earth; for *one* is your Father, which is in Heaven. Neither be called master; for *one* is your Master, even Christ (Matthew 23: 9–10).

Often times one may say, "One and only." This of course is redundant because if there is just "one" it is also the "only". There is "only" one God and He has only "one" people (or nation). Since He was the only one that created and He created us, we are His and belong to no other. "That they may see, and know, and consider, and understand together, that the hand of the Lord has done this, and the Holy One of Israel has created it" (Isaiah 41:20). Recognizing this is an extremely important concept of Scripture! A major part of God's Word to us is to let us know that He is the only one that truly matters (in this universe).

However, we matter to Him as well because He redeemed us (no other) "I, even I, am the Lord; beside me there is no savior. I have declared and have saved..." (Isaiah 43:11-12). We are His people, made for his purpose. Unto all things, God has a purpose. "For the Lord of hosts has purposed, and who shall disannul it? And his hand is stretched out, and who shall turn it back? (Isaiah 14:27) Thus, there are not different "deities" or "paths to Heaven". There is only one of each.

The Number Two (2)

The number *two* represents a difference. It introduces an alternative, contrasting different ideas or ideologies. There cannot be a choice without an alternative from which to choose. In today's language, we would emphasize the word choice. Even during the creation after the first day when God made light on the second day, God separated the light from the darkness. Then Satan deceived Eve, convincing her that there was an alternative to God's directive will. God's absolute directive was that she would die if she ate of the fruit of the tree of knowledge. Satan's response was this: "Surely, you will not die" (Genesis 3:4). The directive was "you will die," but the alternative view was "I will not die."

Enmity can be defined as antagonism, animosity, or even hatred, which implies that there must be an alternative course of thought or action. Satan's course of action was against God, as was Eve's. God, therefore, must deal will Satan as He will with man. "And I will put enmity between you (Satan) and the woman, and between your seed (evil) and her seed (man-Jesus), and it shall bruise your (Satan) head and you shall bruise his (Jesus) heel" (Genesis 3:15). Thus, there was established (in no uncertain terms) for us, the readers of God's Word, that there are *two* possible courses of actions for man. These include good and evil, righteousness and unrighteousness, heaven and hell. Jesus Himself said, "No servant can serve *two* masters: for either he will hate the one, and love the other; or else he will hold to the one, and despise the other. You cannot serve God and mammon" (Luke 16:13). From the beginning, man made the evil choice. This set into motion God's "plan of salvation", thus setting the stage for the need for Bible.

There is the story of Abraham and Lot. For a while, their families lived together. However, after a while, they needed to separate and part ways. A choice needed to be made as to where to live. "And there was strife between the herdsmen of Abram's cattle and Lot's cattle ... And Abram said to Lot, let there be no strife ... separate thyself ... if you will take the left hand, then I will go the right; or if you depart to the right hand, then I will go the left" (Genesis 13:7–9). Thus, a choice of one way or another was made.

There is also this statement regarding *two* opinions by Elijah: "And Elijah came unto all the people and said, How long halt you between *two* opinions? If the Lord be your God, follow Him; but if Baal, then follow him" (1 Kings 18:21).

Recall the story of how God promised Abraham a son (Genesis 15) but Abraham became impatient (human trait) and conceived a child through Hagar, his wife Sarah's handmaiden (Genesis 16). God would still bless Ishmael (the resulting son), but Ishmael was not the son of promise. Ishmael was the result of Abraham's poor human choice.

> Not as though the word of God has taken none effect. For they all are not Israel, which are of Israel. Neither, because they are the seed of Abraham, are they all children; but, in Isaac shall your seed be called. That is, they which are the children of the flesh, these are not the children of God; but the children of the promise are counted for the seed. For this is the word of promise. At this time will come, and Sarah shall have a son. (Romans 9:6–9)

Jacob and Esau were fraternal twins of Isaac and Rebecca. Esau was the firstborn of the twins, and he would have received the inheritance. But he made a poor choice and lost that right. "Lest there be any fornicator, or profane person, as Esau, who for one morsel of meat sold his birthright. For you know that afterward, when he would have inherited the blessing, he was rejected; for he found no place of repentance, though he sought it carefully" (Hebrews 12:16–17). It is an Old Testament story but a New Testament commentary. The history is that man originally made a poor choice and lost eternal life. Mankind lost fellowship with God. But there is a *second* verse to that tune. God, in His infinite wisdom and foreknowledge, knew this would happen. Thus, He created the *second* verse, which is salvation.

It is because of this that the numeric values used by God in His Word help to better explain His character, His position. It is established that there is *one* and only God (the number *one*). Jesus said, "I am the way, the truth, the light. No one comes to the father but by me" (John 14:6). But there is a choice of man, as established by the free will of man. Jesus also discussed the following: "Is it better to build a house in sand … or upon a rock?" (Matthew 7:24–7). That would seem to be a choice!

Although man's God-given free will allows a free choice of these contrasting ideas, God only established one way to attain eternal fellowship with Him in heaven. However, care needs to be given to making choices. To be sure, God made man with free will, meaning that mankind can make choices and is not like a robot whereby man simply acts with no notion of choice. However, the idea of *two* is implying that man would simply choose between God and Satan. But if that were the case, then God and Satan would be on the same plane, and man himself would be a God, having an opportunity to choose God or Satan (on his own), thus becoming a god himself. As mentioned earlier, there is but one God. Thus, although the number *two* does imply choice (one or the other), it goes deeper than that.

Having established the number *two* as contrasting thoughts and having a choice of conflicting ideas, God goes even further in His Word, knowing the poor choices that man makes. Through His love, grace, and mercy, we are able to contemplate a relationship with Him. Jeremiah's lesson of the potter also tells of *God's choice.*

> Arise, and go down to the potter's house, and there I will cause you to hear my words. Then I went down to the potter's house, and behold, he wrought a work on the wheels. And the vessel that he had made of clay was marred in the hand of the potter; so he made it again another vessel, as seemed good to the potter to make it. Then the word of the Lord came to me saying, O house of Israel, cannot I do with you as this potter? says the Lord. Behold, as the clay is in the potter's hand, so are you in My hand, O Israel. (Jeremiah 18:2–6)

Jesus said, "Behold, I stand at the door and knock: if any man hear my voice, and open the door, I will come in to him, and sup with him and him with me" (Revelation 3:20).

Certainly, Israel made some wrong choices. Certainly, we make some wrong choices. But it is God that chooses to love us as opposed to damning us or condemning us because of our sin. In doing so, He would only condemn His own creation … in His own likeness! Thus, God *had* to deal with us accordingly. Instead of mankind falling forever from God, God chose. "For God so loved the world, that He gave His only begotten Son, that whoever believe in Him should not perish, but have everlasting life" (John 3:16).

God created, knowing the frailty of man, and set His plan of salvation in motion at the creation.

> There is one glory of the sun, and another glory of the moon, and another glory of the stars; for one star differs from another in glory. So also is the resurrection of the dead. It is sown in corruption; it is raised in incorruption; it is sown in dishonor; it is raised in glory: it is sown in weakness; it is raised in power: It is sown a natural body; it is raised a spiritual body. There is a natural body, and there is a spiritual body. And so it is written, The first man Adam was made a living soul; the last Adam was made a quickening spirit. The first man is of the earth, earthy: the *second* man is the lord from heaven. (1 Corinthians 15:41-7)

Of course, the *second* man is Jesus. Jesus Himself said that He came not for unison but for division. "Suppose you that I am come to give peace on earth? I tell you, Nay, but rather division" (Luke 12:51). Of course, this leads to the exciting conclusion found at the end of the Bible. "And I saw a new heaven and a new earth; for the first heaven and the first earth were passed away, and there was no more sea" (Revelation 21:1). Seas have long been a separator among the earth, separating people from one continent to another. This division is actually the daily choices of free will that mankind makes each day. People really do choose, but it is God that made the ultimate choice! He chose to create with a plan of salvation.

Other examples of the number two implying choice include the following:

- *Two* birds. One to be killed and one dipped in its blood ... and set free and live (Leviticus 14:4–7).
- *Two* goats (atonement and scapegoat). God judges and God has chosen to redeem, yet judge (Leviticus 16:7).
- *Two* opinions. Follow God or Baal? (1 Kings 18:21).
- Two vessels, one marred but still pliable and able to be shaped into another vessel, or one already hardened and not able to be redefined. Which are you? (Jeremiah 18:1–4).
- Two masters. Which will you follow? (Matthew 6:24).

- Two foundations upon which to build a house. Upon which will you build? (Matthew 7:24).
- Two sons. One does, and one only says. Which are you? (Matthew 21:28–32).
- Two debtors. Which will you be? (Luke 7:41).
- Two men, a Pharisee and a publican going to the temple. Which are you? (Luke 18:10–14).

There are two sides of a coin. There is always comparison. The body is sown in corruption, raised in incorruption. It is sown in dishonor, raised in glory. It is sown in weakness and raised in power. This compares to the following passage: "The body is sown in a natural body and raised a spiritual body" (1 Corinthians 15:42-4). This number *two* transcends the Old and New Testament with unity of meaning.

The Number Three (3)

After one understands the significance of the number one and the number two, one can better understand the numbers *three* and *four.* The number *three* in Scripture represents the spiritual trinity, the completeness and fullness of God, whereas the number *four* represents the physical of man. These numbers are used more than any other number. Not only are they given as individual numbers, but they are also contrasted, comparing to make sure the reader of Scripture knows the difference between an all-everything God and a physical, finite man. *Three* is the number associated with the Godhead, for there are *three* persons in one God as the Father, the Son, and the Holy Spirit (or Holy Ghost). To be sure, God has *three* major attributes. These include omniscience, omnipresence, and omnipotence. Thus, the number *three* denotes divine perfection.

We may know what water is. It is a compound of hydrogen hydroxide. It has but one formula—H_2O. But it can be found in nature in three forms. These include solid ice, liquid water, and gas vapor (or steam). We also have separate attributes, even though we are ourselves one. For example, I am a son, but I am also a father and a husband. Each of these stages or phases has expressed, identifiable characteristics, even though there is unity of the identities.

So it is with God. "Let *us* make man in *our* image, after our likeness" (Genesis 1:26). Notice the pronouns "us" and "our." This would indicate that there is indeed only one God but that He has separate attributes (when needed). This is why throughout the Scripture when praise is given to God in verbal exaltation; the word "holy" is expressed *three* times. "And one cried unto another, and said, Holy, Holy, Holy, is the Lord of hosts. The earth is full of his glory" (Isaiah 6:3). (Notice the three repeats of holy.) There is praise unto Almighty God to the Father, the Son, and the Holy Spirit. "Go you therefore, and teach all nations in the name of the Father, and of the Son, and of the Holy Spirit" (Matthew 28:19). "For there are *three* that bear record in heaven, the Father, the Word (Jesus the Son), and the Holy Ghost and these *three* are *one.* And there are *three* that bear witness on earth, the spirit, and the water, and the blood: and in these *three* agree in *one*" (1 John 5:7–8).

As is illustrated through the number *one,* there is sovereignty of the *one* and only God. In the number *two,* there is contrast, specifically good and evil. In the number *three,* there is the completeness and fullness of God. Even the word "fullness" is remarkable. "The earth is the Lord's and the fullness thereof" (Psalms 24:1). In Genesis 18, we read about *three* angels visiting Abraham and Abraham preparing *three* measures of fine meal. In the fullness of God's redemption, He sent three angels to tell Abraham and Sarah they would have a son from whom the Hebrew nation would arise as well as our Savior, Jesus. God Himself even presents the question: "Is there anything too hard for the Lord?" (Genesis 18:14).

There are those who think that God is merely a God of judgment and pronouncement of all manner of evil because of our transgressions against Him. On the other hand, others think of God as a God who loves and could not allow such evil punishments. Though there is some truth to both concepts, the notion that God unreasonably or ruthlessly punishes some or arbitrarily withholds judgment from some is unfounded. God's message is that we grow to better understand His character and have a better relationship with Him. All else will automatically follow. "And to know the love of Christ, which passes knowledge, that you might be filled with all the fullness of *God*" (Ephesians 3:19). "For in him dwells all the fullness of the *Godhead* bodily" (Colossians 2:9). "Till we all come in the unity of the faith, and of the knowledge of the Son of God, unto a perfect man, unto the measure of the stature of the fullness of *Christ*" (Ephesians 4:13). "And of his fullness have we received grace for grace" (John 1:16).

Thus, the number *three* symbolizes and reinforces the fullness and completeness of the *one* and only God and His nature. David, the man after God's own heart, the lineage from which Jesus came, was anointed three times. The act of anointing was a specific act to symbolize recognition by an established authority, similar to a coronation ceremony. *Three* anointings would illustrate the fullness and completeness of the Godhead who recognized and specifically singled out David. The first anointing was done by Samuel (1 Samuel 16:13). The second anointing was done by the men of Judah (2 Samuel 2:4), and the third was done by the elders of Israel (2 Samuel 5:3).

The following are but a few examples of the oneness of God and *three* attributes of God revealing the fullness or completeness of God.

- *Three* descriptions of God are spoken of in Scripture. They include "God is Light" (1 John 1:5), "God is Love" (1 John 4:8), and "God is Spirit" (John 4:24, Galatians 5:16). God's character is revealed. There is nothing about His character that is lacking!

- *Three* offices of Jesus are named (in His fullness). They are prophet (Ephesians 2:20), priest (Hebrews 4:14), and king (Matthew 2:1). Jesus' nature is described. His person and purpose is complete and full.

- *Three* natures of man (as created by God) are described. They are body, soul, and spirit (1 Thessalonians 5:23). Man's nature as created by God is revealed. In fact, every aspect of created man is complete.

- *Three* of man's greatest enemies as mentioned in Scripture include the following: the World (1 John 2:15–16), the Flesh (Galatians 5:17), and the Devil (Matthew 4:1, 1 John 3:8, John 8:44). These enemies of man are indeed full and complete and lead to the complete and full destruction of man. Yet God in His fullness and completeness is able to overcome ANY enemy of man (His creation)!

- *Three* times the multitudes were fed. They include (2 Kings 4:42–3; Matthew 15:34, 38; Mark 6:38, 44). God's character provides abundantly and completely for His people.

- *Three* times the Hebrews said, "All that the Lord has spoken we will do." At the giving of the law on Mt. Sinai (Exodus 19:8; 24:3, 7), marking the completeness of the covenant between God and man.

- *Three* recorded times, Jesus was tempted by Satan. He was triumphant and had no sin, thus could become the perfect, complete sacrifice (Matthew 4).

- *Three* times, he prayed in the garden of Gethsemane (Mark 14:32–41). Jesus praying three times (not just once) would imply that that the presentation of Jesus toward His purpose of crucifixion was complete and full. No other course of action (by God or any person) would suffice.

- *Three* people were raised from the dead by Jesus, illustrating Jesus' complete and full power (Jairus' daughter in Mark 5, Lazarus in John 11, and a widow's son in Luke 7). The concept that Jesus did have ultimate control over death is illustrated in that Jesus raised three people from the dead (not more or less). Complete control over death illustrates the completeness and fullness of God.

- *Three* hours, darkness preceded Jesus' death on the cross. Thus, when Jesus said, "It is finished," He signified the divinely finished, completed, and perfected the redemptive act of our salvation. It testifies as to our complete sinful plight (darkness) but our complete salvation as Jesus literally took our place and darkness was upon Him (and not us through His redemptive salvation) (Matthew 27:20-6, 45).

- *Three* times is the blessing given in Numbers 6:23–4, depicting the fact that blessings from God are complete and full.
- *Three* major feasts (unleavened bread, weeks, tabernacles) (Deuteronomy 16:16), attributing to the rejoicing and remembrance from whence comes our complete and full joy and salvation.
- *Three* times, the Jordan River was divided, marking the complete and fullness of the miracle and power of God (Joshua 4 and 2 Kings 2:8, 14).
- *Three* things the spies brought from the "Promised Land" (grapes, figs, and pomegranates), which testified to the complete and fullness of the land (Numbers 13:23).
- *Three* children of Anak (Ahiman, Shesai, and Talmai) marked the completeness of the giant power of the enemy that was conquered (Numbers 13:22).
- *Three* people in Scripture God gave a command to "ask of Me" (to Solomon in 1 Kings 3:5, to Ahaz in Isaiah 7:11, and to the Messiah in Psalms 2:8). Jesus implores us all to ask of Him (Matthew 7:7, John 16:23, John 14:13). God the Father, Son, and Holy Spirit is complete and full. On He can supply fully.
- *Three* persons (Peter, James, and John) witnessed the transfiguration of Christ, and including Jesus, the transfiguration included three persons with Moses and Elijah—Jesus, the promised Savior (Messiah), Moses representing the law, and Elijah representing the prophets (Matthew 17).
- *Three* gifts were given at Jesus' birth—gold, frankincense, and myrrh. (Matthew 2.) This illustrates the value and significance of the birth, life, and death of Jesus.

- *Three* gifts of grace from God include faith, hope, and love (1 Corinthians 13:13). Because of love ("the greatest of these is love") and through faith, man has hope (from damnation/condemnation to everlasting life with Him).

- *Three* language inscriptions (Aramaic, Latin, and Greek) were written on the cross to show the completeness of His rejection by man yet universal proclamation that Jesus is indeed "King of the Jews" (John 19:19–20).

- *Three* times did Peter deny Jesus (Matthew 26:69-75), signifying mortal man's complete denial of God. God cannot settle for partial commitment. Nor does He give partial forgiveness or partial judgment.

- *Three* days journey to go into the wilderness to separate His people for a ceremonial service (Exodus 5:3) and depicts the complete separation with which God separated His people from Egypt (which represents sin). The people were to go three days journey away from Egypt, not just one or two days, or more. That number was three. It represented the complete separation that God desired. Upon our salvation, He removes our sin as far as "the east is from the west" and fullness of the Covenant (Psalms 103:12) God cannot associate with sin in any fashion. Thus He must remove Himself completely away from sin or remove sin completely away from Himself.

- *Three* depictions of judgment. Mene mene, tekel, upharsin. Mene: God has numbered your kingdom and finished it. Tekel: You are weighed in the balances and found wanting. Upharsin: "Your kingdom is divided and given to the Medes and Persians" (Daniel 5:25–28.) In the complete judgment of God, sin is weighed (based on the law), and man is found "lacking", and thus the penalty is imposed.

- *Three* days, Jonah was in the belly of the fish, depicting the fullness and completeness of God's action in this instance. (Jonah 1:17) Jonah would eventually go to Nineveh and "preach the gospel" and the "heathen" people of Nineveh did in fact turn to God, illustrating that through the fullness and completeness of God's actions, anyone can come to know Him.

- *Three* days did Jesus spend "in the tomb," dead (Acts 10:40). Jesus did not resurrect or return to life the next day. This may have led to the thought that He never died. Yet unlike Lazarus, He did not stay in the tomb four days either. He was in the tomb *three* days, illustrating that He was completely dead, but He completely conquered death, depicting the complete and fullness of God's actions.

The Number Four (4)

Whereas the number *three* symbolizes divine perfection and reinforces the fullness and completeness of the *one* and only God and His nature, the number *four* signifies the nature of creation, including man. The number *four* represents creation and the fullness and completeness of it as created by God. Yet, because the earth and what is contained in it is physical, it is subject to the physical laws of nature, which include storms, floods, droughts, sicknesses, and diseases. This number illustrates the physical nature of earth and man's pilgrimage through it.

God's message to man through the Scripture contrasts the perfection of His creation (the number three), and His creation is temporarily lost because of sin (the number four) with His power and ability to defeat Satan and redeem His lost creation (man). Certainly in this physical world, there are the four directions: north, east, south, and west. "And he shall send his angels together with a great sound of a trumpet, and they shall gather together his elect from the *four* winds, from one end of heaven to the other" (Matthew 24:31).

But there is also a *fourfold* description of mankind and the physical world in which he lives. In Genesis 1, the literal earth, sun, and moon are referred as coming into physical existence on the fourth day. In Genesis 10, mankind is described as "lands, tongues, families, nations (verse 5); "families, tongues, countries, nations" (verse 20); and "families, tongues, lands, and nations" (verse 31). There are similar listings in Revelation. These include "kindred, tongue, people, nation" (Revelation 5:9); "nations, kindreds, people, tongue" (Revelation 7:9); and "people, kindreds, tongues, nations" (Revelation 11:9). In addition, consider the following:

- The *fourth* commandment refers to the strife of work on the earth. "Remember the Sabbath to keep it holy. Six days shall you labor and do all of your work, but the seventh day is the Sabbath of the Lord; in it you shall not do any work" (Exodus 20:8–10).
- There were *four* persons whose names were changed. They were Abram to Abraham (Genesis 17:5), Sarai to Sarah (Genesis 17:15), Jacob to Israel (Genesis 35:10), and Pashur to Magormissabib (Jeremiah 20:3).
- There are *four* women listed (Matthew 1:3-16) in the genealogy of Jesus. (He was fully God, but He was also fully man.) They are Tamar, Rahab, Ruth, and Bathsheba.
- There are *four* prophetesses listed in the Old Testament. There were Miriam (Exodus 15:20), Deborah (Judges 4:4), Huldah (2 Kings 22:14), and Noadiah (Nehemiah 6:14).
- There are even *four* names of Satan listed in Revelation 20. They are the Dragon (rebellious and apostate), the Old Serpent (seductive), the Devil (accusing), and Satan (personal).
- There is a *fourfold* material blessing in the earth described in Isaiah 60:17. They are the following: "For brass, I will bring gold; for iron I will bring silver; for wood I will bring brass; for stones I will bring iron."
- There is a *fourfold* expression of suffering listed in 2 Corinthians 4:8–9. It is the following: "Troubled but not distressed, perplexed but not in despair. Persecuted but not forsaken, cast down but not destroyed."

- The priests were to take the blood of the sin offering and put it on all *four* corners of the "settle of the altar," depicting the covering of all of man's (earthly) sins (Ezekiel 45:19).

- There are *four* judgments of God. They are the sword, famine, the noisome beast, and pestilence (Ezekiel 14:21).

In Genesis 2 describing the Garden of Eden, there is a single river that departs Eden but is divided into *four* heads as a setting of the world for man. But man must eventually leave the garden. Later in Genesis 10, Abraham is called out of Ur of Chaldees only to find himself (Genesis 14) in a world where *four* kings made war. Abraham would defeat these four kings in the rescue of his nephew, Lot (symbolic of God rescuing man). Later in the book of Revelation, we find there is not a river divided into four heads but only a single river (Revelation 22:1). Thus, the number *four* represents the physical, materialistic world of man, where sin and strife abound, contrasted to the spiritual, righteous, perfect dwelling place of God.

There is a clear distinction between the physical hardships and afflictions that man endures on this earth and the saving grace of God. The Scripture is unmistakable. "But now, in Christ Jesus, you who sometimes were afar off are made nigh by the blood of Christ. For he is our peace, who has made both one, and has broken down the middle wall of partition between us; having abolished the flesh, the enmity, even the law of commandments contained in the ordinances; for to make in himself of twain one new man, so making peace" (Ephesians 2:13–15). "Behold the tabernacle of God of is with men, and he will dwell with them and they shall be his people, and God himself shall be with them, and be their God. And God shall wipe away all tears from their eyes; and there shall be no more sorrow, nor crying, neither shall there be any more pain; for the former things are passed away" (Revelations 21:3–4). What man lost in the beginning of human history is returned at the end human time.

Further review of the number *four* illustrates that the number *four* consists of the numbers *three* and *one* (3 + 1 = 4). It denotes that which follows the revelation of the fullness and completeness of the *one* and only God in the Trinity and it is made manifest in His creative works. It symbolizes the creation, including attributes of earth and of man in his relation to the world. Thus, whereas the number *three* represents divine, infinite fullness and spiritual completeness of the character of God, the number *four* represents the finite material fullness and worldly completeness of His creation, including the trials and tribulations of physical living upon this earth. It is the number of material things that have a beginning but will have an end (for the child of God).

The numbers *three* and *four* contrast this separation and God's character of love, grace, and mercy with His willingness and ability to return to man that which was lost. This contrast is mentioned often in Scripture.

- There are *four* glories listed in 1 Corinthians 15:44.. *Three* are celestial (sun, moon, stars), while the fourth is not detailed and terrestrial.

- The manna given to the wandering Hebrews has a *fourfold* description listed (Exodus 16:14, 31). Three refer to sight or appearance (small, white and round) while one refers to taste (sweet).

- God's witness in the earth has a *fourfold* description listed (Hebrews 2:4). Three are impersonal (signs, wonders, miracles) and one personal (gifts of the Holy Ghost).

The following examples continue to illustrate the number *three* (fullness and completeness of God) contrasted with the number *four* (complete nature of the physical earth and physical man who resides in it) in the Scripture. These expressions were written by more than one author. This further indicates the true authority by which the Bible was inspired, penned, and fitly framed together.

- *Four* specific kinds of flesh are named in the creation. *Three* were animals (birds, beasts or land animals, and fish), and one was man (Genesis 1 and 1 Corinthians 15:39).

- *Four* materials used in the tabernacle. *Three* were metals (gold, silver, and brass) and was nonmetal (Exodus 26:31-7).

- *Four* coverings of the tabernacle are listed. They include animals (goat's hair, ram's skin, and badger's skin), and one was vegetable (fine linen) (Exodus 26:7, 14).

- *Four* ornaments of the curtain in the tabernacle are mentioned. Three were colors blue, purple, and scarlet, and one was a pattern (the cherubim) (Exodus 26:31).

- *Four* houses were built by Solomon, who just happened to be David's *fourth* son born of Bathsheba. *Three* houses were for himself (his "own house" in 1 Kings 7:1, the "house of the forest of Lebanon" in 1 Kings 7:2, the "house" for Pharaoh's daughter in 1 Kings 7:8), and one was the house of God (the temple) (1 Kings 6:37).

- *Four* expressions of transgressions and judgment are written in Amos. Although the message of transgression and imminent judgment is proclaimed throughout the Scripture, it is the way that this message is presented in Amos that is intriguing.

- For *three* transgressions of Damascus, yea for *four,* I will not turn away the punishment thereof (Amos 1:3).

- For *three* transgressions of Gaza, yea for *four,* I will not turn away the punishment thereof (Amos 1:4).

- For *three* transgressions of Tyrus, yea, for *four,* I will not turn away the punishment thereof (Amos1:9).

- Four *three* transgressions of Edom, yea for *four,* I will not turn away the punishment thereof (Amos 1:11).

- For *three* transgressions of Ammon, yea for *four,* I will not turn away the punishment thereof (Amos 1:13).

- For *three* transgressions of Moab, yea for *four,* I will not turn away the punishment thereof (Amos 2:1).

- For the *three* transgressions of Judah, yea for *four,* I will not turn away the punishment thereof (Amos 2:4).
- For the *three* transgressions of Israel, yea for *four,* I will not turn away the punishment thereof (Amos 2:6).

Consider the story of the *four* beasts of Nebuchadnezzar's dream in Daniel 2. The *four* beasts that are described are divided into *three* plus *one,* where the one stands out in contrast to the other three. *Three* were made of metals (gold, silver, brass), and *one* was a mixture of metal and mire (iron and clay). Again in Daniel 7, his vision of *four* beasts is described similarly. The first *three* wild beasts are *named* (lion, bear, leopard), while the fourth is only described and *not named.* However, this unnamed beast was "dreadful and terrible and exceedingly strong."

Of course, this is the prophecy of the *four* world kingdoms that include Babylon, Persia, Greece, and the Roman Empire. Jerusalem was conquered in 586 BC, the temple destroyed and Hebrews carried away in to captivity. Persia was the next world power that allowed the Hebrews to return and rebuild the temple. As the years passed, the Hebrews fell under the influence and dominance of the Greeks (the New Testament being written primarily in Greek), culminating in times of Roman authority (the fourth beast) when Jesus was crucified and when the rebuilt temple completely was destroyed in 70 AD.

There are other contrasts that can be made between the numbers three and four, especially with regards to lineage. These will be discussed later.

The Number Five (5)

Quickly following the establishment of *one* (only one God), *two, three,* and *four* (God's perfection, even in creation) we come to the number *five.* Summing one and four is five, or summing two and three is still *five.* God and God alone (by choice) created a physical and spiritual world. God and God alone dispenses His grace. By definition, sin is sin, and anything associated with it is sin. Therefore, anything that is of sin cannot be used for salvation to save from sin. "For the wages of sin is death" (Romans 3:23).

The physical world is insufficient in and of itself for its salvation. Thus, the implication of the use of the number five is not sufficient of itself but needs something else. Oftentimes the numbers three and four seem emphasized, but the number *five* is significant because something else is needed. Man was created with *five* toes and *five* fingers, yet these physical attributes are not sufficient enough. The woman at the well had *five* husbands, yet they were not enough to satisfy her (John 4:18). They were not sufficient. They did not satisfy her. Therefore, the number *five* illustrates that although we have much, we are still in need. And though we think we are satisfied, we are not. Although we think we are all right, we are in need of God (Christ) to save us. Only God is sinless. Therefore, only God can save that which is lost.

God so saves because of His love. Thus, His expression of that love is grace ... through His Son, Jesus, "but the gift of God is eternal life through Jesus Christ out Lord" (Roman 3:23). God's physical world requires salvation, and through His grace, it is offered. And by choice, man can accept ... or reject. Man's (the world) attempts at salvation are insufficient. Grace must be accomplished through God and God alone. The number *five* represents God's grace. "For by grace you are saved through faith; and that not of yourselves; it is a gift of God; Not of works, lest any man should boast" (Ephesians 2:8–9). So it can be seen that man's eternal destiny is established by God's grace, but how does the number *five* fit in?

God had predetermined that the Messiah would come from the lineage of Abraham, Isaac, and Jacob. More specifically, the Messiah would come from the tribe of Judah (prophesied in Genesis 49 and listed in Matthew 1:3). It was Judah that had *five* sons, but it was Jesus that gave salvation.

Mankind thinks and attempts to do things on his own without understanding that God is ultimately in control. Man is constantly working on his own behalf, taking and receiving gifts, doing works in the hopes that it will "all work out." In other words, the working out and outcomes of situations of man are thought of as simply doing the good work and the good end will occur. Part of God's message as embedded in the number *five* is that especially regarding our salvation or "final outcome" cannot be attained by our own account. What we do (of our own) is not enough. More is need. In fact, so much more is needed that we cannot of our own accords achieve it.

It was after they had taken the ark from the Israelites that the five Philistine lords desired to return it (after they experienced some rather nasty consequences). So they returned the ark with additional gifts of five golden emrods and five golden mice, one for each lord (1 Samuel 6). The Philistines so desired to be placed in a better light, to be rid of the hardships they were experiencing as a result of mocking the God of Israel. In their eyes they believed their gifts were enough to pacify the God of the Hebrews. In the long run, it was not! As hard as it may seem to imagine and comprehend, there is no amount of "good" man can do of his own accord that can please (or pacify) God.

When young David killed Goliath, he picked up *five* stones (to put in his bag to fight the giant). Many have wondered why David picked up *five* stones if he was only going to need one. Some have said he did so because Goliath had four brothers (or sons). Another view is that it was God who gave the victory by grace. It was God and only God who gives salvation. "This day will the Lord deliver you into my hand; and I will smite you, and take your head from you ... and all this assembly shall know that the Lord saves not with a sword and spear: for the battle is the Lord's, and he will give you into our hands" (1 Samuel 17:46–7). Certainly David would not use all five stones. But he picked up five, not ten or even one. No number of stones or (even David who would use them) would be enough. It was God who saved, not David. It was God who killed Goliath, not David.

As King Saul was trying to kill David, David fled to *five* different places (Nob, Gath, the cave of Adullam, the forest of Hereth, and the wilderness of Ziph) to escape death. In Nob, David asked the priest for *five* loaves of bread, but the priest did not have them. It was God's intervention that saved David, not he himself.

In addition, as King Saul and his son, Jonathon, were being killed in Jezreel, "And Jonathan, Saul's son, had a son that was lame of his feet. He was *five* years old when the tidings came of Saul and Jonathan out of Jezreel, and his nurse took him up and fled, that he fell and became lame. And his name was Mephibosheth" (2 Samuel 4:4). David committed to "looking out" for Mephibosheth following the death of Jonathon (2 Samuel 9:1-13). David restores land to Mephibosheth and later David literally spared Mephibosheth's life when an issue arose with the Gibeonites (2 Samuel 21: 1-7). Thus, Mephiboseth was the recipient of commitment and grace by King David.

After the Israelites left the bondage of Egypt, they traveled in the wilderness. An ark (of the covenant) was made according to God's specifications in which to place His laws. "And you shall put the mercy seat above upon the ark; and in the ark you shall put the testimony that I shall give you. And there will I meet with you, and I will commune with you from above the mercy seat" (Exodus 25:21–2). But above this arc with the mercy seat were two cherubim. "And you shall make two cherubim of gold, of beaten work, shall you make them, in the two ends of the mercy seat" (Exodus 25:18).

There are laws and rules of living that are presented to man by God. The laws and rules are at least known by man and so man can be held accountable for the keeping or breaking of these laws. However, God is also aware that because of the sinful nature of man, man is unable to keep these laws. So, literally, these laws were placed in the Arc of the Covenant but were covered over by the mercy seat where the spiritual aspect of God is represented by the cherubim.

They were instructed by God to build a tabernacle. The tabernacle represents the dwelling place of God. But because God is holy and mankind is not, man could not exactly be in the direct (physical) presence of almighty God at this juncture. Thus, God instructed them to construct a tabernacle or symbolic temporary dwelling place among His people. This temporary dwelling place of God was not sufficient. Of course, the temple was later built (though later destroyed as well). But the Bible is also explicit in explaining what the temple of God truly is. "Jesus answered them and said unto them, Destroy this temple (His body) and in three days I will raise it up" (John 2:19). "What? do you not know that your body is the temple (dwelling place) of the Holy Spirit, which is in you, which you have of God, and you are not your own" (1 Corinthians 6:19). Here on earth amidst deceit and sin, physical things are not enough ... for our total completion.

Therefore, as part of the construction of the physical tabernacle, its inclusions are described as follows:

> The *five* curtains shall be coupled together one to another; and the other *five* curtains shall be coupled one to another. And you shall make base of acacia wood; *five* for the boards of the west side of the tabernacle, and *five* bars for the boards for the side of the tabernacle; for the two sides westward. And you shall make an altar of acacia wood, *five* cubits long, and *five* cubits wide. (Exodus 26:3; 26-27; 27:1)

Then in the book of Revelation 21:3, we read, "Behold the tabernacle of God is with men, and He shall dwell with them and they shall be His people and God Himself shall be with them, and be their God."

Try as we will, we cannot come to God and commune with Him on our own. Only through the actions of God can that happen. The number *five* alludes to this. Only by God's grace can that happen.

The anointing oil (for priests) contained *five* parts—myrrh, cinnamon, calamus, cassia, and olive oil (Exodus 30:23–5). But it is God who receives us (through His Son, Jesus) and anoints us with His Holy Spirit.

> But as it is written, Eye has not seen, nor ear has not heard, neither have entered into the heart of man, the things which God has prepared for then that love Him. But God has revealed them unto us by His Spirit for the Spirit searches all things, yea the deep things of God ... Now we have received not the spirit of the world, but the spirit which is of God, that we might know the things that are freely given to us of God. (1 Corinthians 2:9–12)

When Solomon built the temple once again, it and the furnishings were built according to God's specifications.

> And within the oracle he (Solomon) made two cherubim of olive tree, each ten cubits high. And *five* cubits was the one wing of the cherub, and *five* cubits the other wing of the

> cherub: from the uttermost part of one wing to the uttermost part of the other ... And the entering of the oracle he made doors of olive tree; the lintel and side posts were a *fifth* part of the wall. (1 Kings 6:23–4, 31)

God allows us to come to Him through grace. Thus, nothing we do of ourselves is sufficient.

When Jesus fed the *five* thousand, He used the *five* loaves. However, He *also* used two fish in this instance as well. With the two fish, as they sat in fifties, Jesus fed them to completeness (Luke 9:10–17). The number two contrasts. And we must add choice to this illustration. Jesus also said, "It is written that man shall not live by bread alone" (Matthew 4:4). Thus, man's wishes and even desires are not enough to allow us to have an everlasting fellowship with a Holy God.

As the rich man was tormented in hell (Luke 16), he desired to testify to his *five* brothers about his plight. But he was told that his coming back from the dead would not be sufficient for his brothers. They would not believe.

However, God does desire a relationship. That desire and ability gives us the availability to an everlasting relationship with God. Simply stated, it is through God's grace that we can have this relationship, and the number *five* illustrated this character of God in Scripture.

The Numbers Six (6)

The number *six* is the number of imperfection. It represents man in his current imperfect state, and it represents his rebellion and disobedience. It signifies the worship and works of man, which are not perfect. It is the number of man, imperfect and destitute without God (without Christ). The world was created in six days. Only on the seventh (Sabbath) was there finality and completeness of God's creation. Man was created on the *sixth* day (Genesis 1: 26–31), and the Bible says, "Six days shall you labor" (Exodus 20:9). The number *six* (and its derivatives) is used nearly 300 times in the Bible. It marks secular incompleteness and indicates man's sinful nature, which is incomplete without God. It is a number that falls short of the perfection God.

- Cain's genealogy is the first biblical illustration of the number *six*. His genealogy is given through the *sixth* generation (Genesis 4:17–24) and falls short of the genealogy listed through that of Seth to Christ (Luke 3:23–38). (Genealogies will be discussed in a later chapter.) Thus Cain's genealogy "is not perfect". It is human.

- Abraham is listed as interceding on behalf of Sodom *six* times (Genesis 18) and fell short of the Divine Intercessor. (God destroyed Sodom.)

- There were *six* years of usurpation of the throne of David by Athalia (2 Kings 11:1-3). She thought her actions were complete. But Joash was actually spared, and in the seventh year, the throne of David continued in perfection through him.

- The burnt offering is mentioned *six* times in Genesis 22. (The seventh offering would be a divine substitute that God Himself would provide.)

- *Six* earthquakes are mentioned in the Bible. They are found in Exodus 19:18, 1 Kings 19:11, Amos 1:1, Zechariah 14:5, Matthew 27:54 and 28:2, and Acts 16:26. These were usually in association with judgment. But these are nothing compared to the final judgment.

- *Six* times, Jesus was asked for a (physical) sign. They include the Pharisee (Matthew 12:38), the Sadducees (Matthew 16:1), the disciple, (Matthew 24:3), the people (Luke 11:16), the Jews (John 2:18), and the people again (John 6:30). All of the physical signs of this earth cannot express who God is. It certainly goes a long way, but there is more to come for the one who in earnest wishes to "find God".

- *Six* persons bore testimony to the Savior's innocence. They include Pilate (Luke 23:14), Herod (Luke 23:15), Pilate's wife (Matthew 27:19), Judas (Matthew 27:3), the dying thief (Luke 23:41), and the centurion (Luke 23:47). Although Jesus was completely innocent, He was still guilty of sin (of our sin)!

- *Six* hours, Jesus hung on the cross (Mark 15:25, 34). Although hard to comprehend, the sacrificial (sinless) Jesus who hung on the cross and died for our sins was as imperfect and "sinful" as could possibly be as He took upon Himself our sins and imperfections.

The Number Seven (7)

In contrast to the meaning of the number six (imperfection), the number *seven* represents the perfection of God. Whereas the number *three* illustrates the completeness and *fullness* of God, the number *seven* marks the completeness and *perfection* of God. God is perfect in every sense of the word. He is complete in all that He does. He is also perfect in that which He does. Thus, the number *seven* represents spiritual perfection. It is mentioned almost four hundred times in the Old Testament alone and more than five hundred times in the entire Bible. It occurs forty-two times in the books of Daniel (Old Testament) and Revelation (New Testament) alone. The Hebrew word for *seven* is *sheva,* and it comes from the root *savah,* which means "to be full, have enough, to be satisfied." This is what the number *seven* means—perfect.

Because of the nature of man, it is difficult to comprehend and understand the very nature of "perfect". We may think we understand perfection, but its concept may truly go "over our heads". For example, in the game of baseball there may be a "no-hitter" thrown by a pitcher, in which no opposing player got a legitimate hit and the headlines and news would spread. A "perfect-game" on the other hand means that of the 27 batters that could step into the batter's box, no one even got on base, either by a hit, error or walk. This would seem perfect and is actually proclaimed as a perfect game. But what about a baseball game in which a pitcher **strikes out** all 27 batters. No one even grounds out or flies out. And to be honest, we could not even imagine a Major League baseball pitcher striking out every batter he faced in a game... throughout his entire career! Every game that he pitched, he struck out every batter. Now that would be perfection!

What about a basketball player that never missed a shot, never? Or what about in the sport of football a quarterback who never threw an incomplete pass, never, in his entire career? We may comprehend good...or even very good. But we find it difficult to imagine and comprehend perfection. Thus, to fully express and proclaim what complete, fullness or perfection truly means, the Bible give us the numeric expression to better understand and comprehend.

The concept of the completeness and perfection of God using the number *seven* in the Bible begins in Genesis. Of course, the earth was created in six days, but on the *seventh* day, God rested (as if God really needs to rest). But it demonstrates the fullness and completeness of creation. There is nothing left to do. We may have our various projects that we may finish. But then we are always trying to "make it better" or redo bits and pieces. Otherwise, we are never really satisfied with our completed project.

With the sanctification of the Sabbath (*seventh*), all aspects of God's creation are perfected and completed in the number *seven*. Enoch was the seventh from God ... and did not die. He was taken (Genesis 5:24). Methuselah was *seven* generations from Adam and was Enoch's son, and he was the longest living human ever (Genesis 5:27). Lamech, father of Noah was *seven* generations from Seth (Adam's next born after Cain and Abel), the directive lineage of Jesus, and he lived to be *777* (*three instances of seven*) years old (Genesis 5:31). After Methuselah's death, God waited *seven* days and began the flood (Genesis 7:4). Noah took the animals by *sevens* (male and female) into the arc for salvation (Genesis 7:2). The arc rested in the *seventh* month after the flood (Genesis 8:4). Yet it stayed another *seven* days and sent forth the dove (Genesis 8:10, 12). Thus, following the creation, the fall and the salvation of man by Christ is seen through the story of the salvation of Noah's family from the Flood. The salvation is complete and perfect.

In the book of Leviticus, we find a continuation of this thought. "And the Lord spake unto Moses in mount Sinai ... Six years will you sow the field, and six years will you prune your vineyard and gather in the fruit thereof; But in the *seventh* year shall a Sabbath of rest unto the land, a Sabbath for the Lord: you will neither sow your field, nor prune your vineyard: (Leviticus 25:1–4). In addition, there was to be a "jubilee year."

> And you shall have *seven* Sabbaths of years unto you, *seven* times *seven* years; and the space of the seven Sabbaths shall be unto you forty and nine years. Then you shall cause the trumpet of the jubilee to sound on the tenth day of the *seventh* month, in the day of atonement shall you make the trumpet sound throughout all you land. And you shall hallow the fiftieth year. And proclaim liberty throughout the land ... for it is the jubilee; it shall be holy unto you. (Leviticus 25:8-10)

Thus, because of the sacrifice of Christ (atonement), there is cause and reason for rest and security to come.

It is amazing that in Matthew 24:31, we find, "And he shall send his angels and with a great sound of the trumpet, and they shall gather his elect from the four winds, from one end of the heaven to the other." And in 1 Thessalonians 4:16–17, we find, "For the Lord himself shall descend from heaven with a shout, with the voice of the archangel, with the trump of God: and the dead in Christ shall rise first: Then we which are alive and remain shall be caught up together with them in the clouds, to meet the lord in the air: and so shall we ever be with the Lord." And in Revelation 8:6, we read, "And the seven angels which had the seven trumpets prepared themselves to sound."

Thus, from the Old Testament to the New Testament, we can see that there will be an ultimate perfection that comes to fruition. There is the story of an incident between Abraham and Abimelech.

> And Abraham reproved Abimelech because of a well of water, which Abimelech's servant had violently taken away. And Abimelech said I do not know who has done this thing: neither have I heard of it until you have told me today. And Abraham took sheep and oxen, and gave them unto Abimelech and both of them made a covenant. And Abraham set *seven* ewe lambs of the flock by themselves. And Abimelech said unto Abraham, What do you mean by these *seven* ewe lambs which you have set by themselves? And he said, For these *seven* ewe lambs will you take of my hand, that they may be a witness unto me, that I have digged this well. (Genesis 21:25–30)

Following this in the New Testament is a story of Jesus speaking to a Samaritan woman at a well. "Jesus answered and said unto her, Whoever drinks of this water shall thirst again: But whoever drinks of the water that I shall give him shall never thirst again: but the water that I shall give him shall be in him a well of water springing up into everlasting life" (John 4:13–14).

Jacob served Laban *seven* years for Rachel (his first love) "because he loved her" (Genesis 29:20). Pharaoh's dream, interpreted by Joseph, had *seven* well-nourished cows and *seven* malnourished cows and *seven* good ears of corn and *seven* bad ears of corn in it (Genesis 41:1-6). There were *seven* years of plenty and *seven* years of famine in Egypt (Genesis 41:53-4).

In Leviticus 14, we find the cleansing of lepers. There were two birds taken. One was killed, and the other dipped in its blood. To those who had leprosy, they were sprinkled with the blood *seven* times ... and were made clean and whole.

The ark, taken by the Philistines, remained in their custody for seven month, and of course, it had all kinds of problems. Thus, it was in the completion of time (that is *seven* months later, not one, two or ten months later), that they focused on returning the ark back to the Israelites (1 Samuel 6). This timing was "perfect" as it took this long for them to see the arc as an instrument from God. It may take man a while to fully see God, but in the completion and perfection of God's timing, man will certainly find out. "Every knee shall bow and every tongue shall confess to God" (Romans 14:11, quoted from Isaiah 45:23).

This concept of the completion or perfection of not only time, but any aspect of God continues even through the book of Revelation with *seven* churches (1:4), *seven* spirits (1:4), *seven* golden candlesticks (1:12), *seven* stars (1:16), *seven* angels (1:20) *seven* lamps (4:5), *seven* seals (5:5), *seven* horns (5:6), *seven* eyes (5:6), *seven* trumpets (8:2), *seven* thunders (10:3), *seven* heads (12:3), *seven* crowns (12:3), *seven* plagues (15:1), *seven* golden vials (15:7), *seven* mountains (17:9), and *seven* kings (17:10). Thus, the idea of a perfect love, a very real (perfect) condemnation, and a (perfect) salvation is written again and again in the perfect text we call the Bible.

It took *seven* years for Solomon to complete the building of the temple in Jerusalem. The very presence of God is perfect. The entire contents of the Bible, the stories, the messages, all of it had to be accomplished in order to express the completeness and fullness of God. Everything aspect of God including His nature and His actions are "perfect".

Other brief expressions of the number *seven* found in the Old Testament and New Testament include the following and illustrate perfection:

- *Seven* Daughters of Jethro (Exodus 2:16).
- *Seven* days of eating unleavened bread (Exodus 23:15).
- *Seven* sprinkles of blood (Leviticus 4:6).
- *Seven* lamps for the tabernacle (Leviticus 23:42).
- *Seven* lamps (Numbers 8:2).
- *Seven* nations (Deuteronomy 7:1).
- *Seven* priests with seven trumpets on the seventh day (Joshua 6:4).
- *Seven* days of feasting for Samson (Judges 14:17).
- *Seven* locks of Samson's hair (Judges 16:13).
- *Seven* times, Naaman dipped himself in the Jordan River (2 Kings 5:14).
- *Seven* sneezes (2 Kings 4:35).
- *Seven* loaves of bread (Matthew 15:34).
- *Seven* brothers (Mark 12:20).
- *Seven* demons of Mary Magdalene (Luke 8:2).
- *Seven* sons of the priest (Acts 19:14).
- *Seven* sayings did Christ speak from the cross.

In the book of Genesis we find that God "finished" creating the world in six days, but included the seventh day of "rest" (Did God really need to rest?) before establishing the "completeness" of his creation. It implies that that God gives more than just life. He gives meaning to that life. The sixth saying of Jesus as He hung on the cross was, "It is finished (or completed)" (John 19:30). However, the seventh and final saying Jesus spoke from the cross was, "Father, into your hands I commend my spirit" (Luke 23:46). Although Jesus exclaimed, "It is finished," it also had to be established that He did it. He "gave" His life. No one took it from Him. After the virgin birth and perfect life, and after the beating and humiliating crucifixion, Jesus literally, physically and of His own volition died. Since He was perfect, how can another take life (or anything for that matter) from Him? The other sayings of Jesus on the cross are found in Matthew 27:46, Luke 23:34, Luke 23:43, and John 19:26, 28.

Everything—and without exception—everything of God is perfect. By definition, if *anything* were not perfect, then God could not be God. Throughout Scripture at the outset in the book of Genesis until the end in the book of Revelations, all aspects of God's Word must be perfect, or there would be no other God.

The Number Eight (8)

The number *eight* is associated with new beginnings. Following the sin of Adam, God set in motion His redemptive plan. Of course, there was the separation of Cain from the lineage of Adam, and salvation (Jesus) would come through Seth. Noah is the *eighth* generation from Seth, so following sin and death, there comes a new beginning. In addition, though there may have been many animals on the arc, there were only *eight* people (souls) who were saved (from the flood), specifically Noah (which was the *eighth* person) and his three sons and their wives (Genesis 7:7, 1 Peter 3:20, and 2 Peter 2:5).

The music scale contains seven notes. The *eighth* note begins a new scale. Circumcision was to be performed on the *eighth* day (Genesis 17:12). Jesus' family followed this as Jesus was circumcised on the *eighth* day (Luke 2:21). Jesus was no longer in His glory in

Heaven. He was human on earth. In essence a new beginning for all of mankind and God's purpose comes to fruition through Jesus. After the resurrection, Jesus waited *eight* days to appear before all his disciples again, including Thomas who previously doubted that Jesus had indeed resurrected (John 20:26). These indicate a new beginning… of a life for all of the disciples.

In the cleansing of a person with leprosy, the priest would take two birds, kill one, dip the other in its blood, and then sprinkle the blood on the person with leprosy. However, on the *eighth* day, the priest would take two lambs, offer a trespass and atonement offering, and cleanse the person of leprosy, thereby creating a new beginning for the afflicted person (Leviticus 14).

David was the *eighth* son of Jesse (1 Samuel 17:12, 14). Thus, in His infinite wisdom and foreknowledge, God knew of a new beginning through David, who would become not only a physical kin of Israel but the ancestor the King of Kings, Jesus, giving the fallen man a new beginning.

Aeneas, a man of palsy for *eight* years, was given a new life after he was healed (Acts 9:33–5). Concerning dedications and offerings, the oxen and sheep were to remain with their mothers for seven days, but on the *eighth* day, they were to be given to God (Exodus 22:30).

At the time of the Babylonian takeover of Jerusalem, Jehoiachin was king. It was in King Jehoiachin's *eight* year of reign that Nebuchadnezzar; King of Babylon carried him, as well as Temple treasures away. This ended the nation of Judah and began the Babylonian exile. Once again, it illustrates a new beginning (at least for the remaining nation of Israel called Judah (2 Kings 24:11–17).

As the previous days of our lives depict sin, doom, and no hope, there is coming a new day when we will have a new life. You shall not delay to offer the first of your ripe fruits, and of your liquors, the first-born of your sons shall you give unto me … on the *eighth* day you shall give it me (Exodus 22:29–30). "And from Jesus Christ, who is the faithful witness, and the first begotten of the dead, and the prince of the kings of the earth. Unto him that loved us, and wash us from our sins in his own blood" (Revelation 1:5). "And you shall circumcise the flesh of you foreskin; and it shall be a token of the covenant that is between me and you. And he that is *eight* days old shall be circumcised among you, every male child in your generations, he that is born in the house, or bought with money of any stranger, which is not of your seed" (Genesis 17:11–12). "In whom you are circumcised with the circumcision made without hands, in putting off the body of the sins of the flesh by the circumcision of Christ" (Colossians 2:11). This is connected to a new creation through Christ. "Therefore we are buried with him by baptism into death: that like as Christ was raised up from the dead by the glory of the Father, even so we also should walk in newness of life" (Romans 6:4).

There are *eight* specific accounts, (not three, five or any other number) of individual resurrections recorded in the Bible. These include three in the Old Testament and five in the New Testament. Even here, notice the number three in the Old Testament testifying to the Father, Son and Holy Spirit of a Holy and complete God (Father, Son, Holy Spirit or creator, redeemer, sustainer), and the number five of the New Testament signifying the grace of God supplied through Jesus (sacrificial lamb, savior). Obviously, these previously dead individuals got new beginnings. These include the following:

- Elijah raises the son of a woman (1 Kings 17:8–9, 17–23).
- Elisha raises the son of a Shunammite woman (2 Kings 4:16–20, 32–6).
- God uses the bones of Elisha to raise a man back to life (2 Kings 13:20–21).
- Jesus resurrects the only son of a woman from Nain (Luke 7:11–15).
- Jesus raises the daughter of Jarius from the dead (Mark 5:35–42).
- Jesus raises Lazarus from the dead (John 11:1–46).
- Peter raises a generous woman named Tabitha (Dorcus) from the dead (Acts 9:36-41).
- Paul raises a young man named Eutychus from the dead (Acts 20:9–12).

The Number Nine (9)

The number *nine* has been associated with finality, and it is often associated with a finality of judgment when it is used in Scripture. The term judgment means final decision, not necessarily a pronouncement of a bad or wicked outcome but simply the finality of the outcome. "And about the ninth hour, Jesus cried with a loud voice, saying, Eli, Eli, lama sabach-thani? That is to say, My God, My God, why have you forsaken me?" (Matthew 27:46). God had previously pronounced judgment on sin, or the penalty of sin and the finality of the Jesus was the payment for that sin. Essentially, Jesus became sinful at that moment, receiving our sins, thus separating Him from the Father. However, contained within that judgment was the power of Christ overcoming death.

God established the finality of His covenant with Abraham when Abraham was ninety-nine years old. Of course, at this point in history, Abraham was chosen (choice from the number two and thus two nines) to establish the finality and the end of sin with the lineage and redemptive process through the Hebrews (Judah) and Jesus.

This concept of finality is also identity—that is, we belong to God and the finality of His creation and identity. Thus, there are *nine* gifts of the spirit. They include the following: 1) word of wisdom, 2) word of knowledge 3) faith, 4) healing, 5) miracles, 6) prophecy, 7) discerning of spirits, 8) tongues, 9) discerning of tongues (1 Corinthians 12:8–10). But the gifts of the spirit are not to be confused with the fruit of the spirit, which include the following: 1) love, 2) joy, (3) peace, 4) longsuffering, 5) gentleness, 6) goodness, 7) faith, 8) meekness, 9) temperance (Galatians 5:22–3). These are all part of God's ultimate plan.

However, much of the number *nine* is associated with the finality of judgment upon man. After Adam sinned, Noah became the *ninth* generation from Adam. Other finality judgment illustrations include these: "In the *ninth* year of Hoshea the king of Assyria took Samaria, and carried Israel away into Assyria ... For so it was, that the Children of Israel had sinned against the Lord their God" (2 Kings 17:6–7). "And it came to pass in the *ninth* year of his reign, in the tenth month, that Nebuchadnezzar, king of Babylon came, he and all his host, against Jerusalem, and pitched against it; and they built forts against it round about. And the city was besieged unto the eleventh year of King Zedekiah (of Judah). And on the *ninth* day of the fourth month the famine prevailed in the city, and there was no bread for the people of the land. And the city was broken up" (2 Kings 25:1–4). In each instance, the northern kingdom of Israel was judged, and the finality of the judgment came to fruition. And it was the same with the southern kingdom of Judah. There is finality.

Scripture does pronounce judgment. Haggai 1:11 mentions *nine* particular judgments.

1. And I called for a drought upon the land,
2. And upon the maintains,
3. And upon the corn,
4. And upon the new wine,
5. And upon the oil,
6. And upon that which brings forth,
7. And upon men,
8. And upon cattle,
9. And upon all the labor of the hands.

The point of the number *nine* is the idea that God's plan and God's work is final and just. It is a conclusion of a whole matter so far as divine things are concerned. God created life perfect, but man sinned and became imperfect and died. But God had a plan of salvation for man and destruction for all sin, including death itself (the wages of sin). Thus, even as the beginning was perfect, so shall the end. But from the creation and course of human events through time, so shall it conclude as pronounced and purposed in the exact timing and ways within the will of the divine God who did it all. But *nine* is also the square of three, and three is the number of divine perfection as well as the number peculiar to the Holy Spirit. It is not surprising, therefore, to find that this number denotes finality in divine things.

The following are but a few miscellaneous illustrations. In each case, one part of their lives ended, and they had new beginnings.

Nine persons were *stoned.*

1. The blasphemer (Leviticus 24:14)
2. The Sabbath-breaker (Numbers 15:36)
3. Achan (Joshua 7:25)
4. Abimelech (Judges 9:53)
5. Adoram (1 Kings 12:18)
6. Naboth (1 Kings 21:10)
7. Zechariah (2 Chronicles 24:21)
8. Stephen (Acts 7)
9. Paul (Acts 14:19)

Nine persons were afflicted with *blindness.*

1. The men at Lot's door (Genesis 19:11)
2. Isaac (Genesis 27:1)
3. Jacob (Genesis 48:10)
4. Samson (Judges 16:21)
5. Eli (1 Samuel 4:15)
6. The prophet Ahijah (1 Kings 14:4)
7. The Syrian Army (2 Kings 6:18)
8. King Zedekiah (2 Kings 25:7)
9. Elymas (Acts 13:11)

Nine were afflicted with *leprosy.*

1. Moses (Exodus 4:6)
2. Miriam (Numbers 12:10)
3. Naaman (2 Kings 5:1)
4. Gehazi (2 Kings 5:27)

5–8. The four lepers at Samaria (2 Kings 7:3)

9. Azariah (2 Kings 15:5)

Nine widows are especially mentioned.

1. Tamar (Genesis 38:19)
2. Woman of Tekoah (2 Samuel 14:5)
3. Hiram's mother (1 Kings 7:14)
4. Zeruah (1 Kings 11:26)
5. Woman of Zarephath (1 Kings 17:9)
6. The poor widow (Mark 12:42)
7. Anna (Luke 2:37)
8. Widow of Nain (Luke 7:12)
9. The persistent widow (Luke 18:3)

The Number Ten (10)

The number *ten* represents divine order or ordinal perfection. However, it should not be confused with the number seven. With respect to God's total creation, both physical and spiritual, everything is in perfect order. Even regarding what seems to be evil, sin, and bad things, God is in complete control. Nothing is lacking or wanting.

Although there may be sin and there is human failure, in His character, God has that in order and within His provision. "In all matter of wisdom and understanding that the king inquired of them he found them *ten* times better than all the magicians and astrologers who were in all his realm" (Daniel 1:20).

It is interesting to note that when reflecting upon the overall creation of God and the redemption and plan of salvation of God through Jesus, including the writing of the Scripture to reveal this to man, all of this dictates considerable arrangement, injunction and order. This divine order can be seen through the number *ten*. Consider the following illustration in Exodus 30:12–13.

> When you take the sum of the children of Israel after their number, then shall they give every man a ransom for his soul unto the Lord, when you number them; that there be no plague among them, when you number them. They will give, every one that passes among them that are numbered, half a shekel, after the shekel of the sanctuary: (a shekel is twenty gerahs) (thus a half shekel is ten gerahs) shall be the offering of the Lord.

God had originally pronounced that all of the firstborn Hebrew males belonged to Him. So it seemed that every Hebrew male over the age of twenty had to pay ten gerahs as a ransom (atonement money). But after He took them out of Egypt He declared He would have the Levites instead of the firstborn Hebrews. However, so both (groups) could be redeemed, God ordered Moses and Aaron to take a census of the Levites and the firstborn of the rest of Hebrews.

> And I (God), behold I have taken the Levites from among the children of Israel instead of all the first born that opens the womb among the children of Israel: Therefore the Levites shall be mine ... And you shall take the Levites for me (I am the Lord) instead of all the firstborn among the children of Israel ... And all the first-born males by the number of names, from a month old and upward, of those that were numbered were

> twenty and two thousand and threescore and thirteen. And the Lord spoke unto Moses, saying, Take the Levites instead of all the first born among the children of Israel ... And for those that are to be redeemed of the two hundred and threescore and thirteen of the first born of the children of Israel, which are more than the Levites, then you shall take five shekels apiece by the poll, after the shekel of the sanctuary ... is to be redeemed unto Aaron and to his sons. And Moses took the redemption money of them that were above them that were redeemed by the Levites. Of the first-born of the children of Israel he took a thousand three hundred and threescore and five shekels ... And Moses gave the money of them that were redeemed unto Aaron and to his sons according to the word of the Lord. (Numbers 3:13, 43–51)

Looking more closely at this we find that after the numbering or census, it was found that that there were 22,273 firstborn males (Hebrews), but there were only 22,000 Levites. This meant that there were 273 more firstborn of Israel than there were Levites. Mathematically, 1,365 shekels (twenty gerahs per shekel) is equals to 27,300 gerahs. If 27,300 gerahs is divided by the 273 firstborns (more than the Levites), this is equal to 100 gerahs). And the 100 gerahs (Numbers 3:50) is *ten* times more than the 10 gerahs (Exodus 30:13) that was the ransom price to be paid. So, the 273 (more than the Levites) of the children of Israel wound up having to pay *ten* times the ransom money, which amounted to 1,365 shekels. It is not the magnitude or specific amount of money that is important, but the concept that there is an amount and it is sufficient and it is derived from a divine plan. What other text would go through this type of math, and for what purpose?

The ramifications go deeper than even this. Literally, this illustration simply showed that all (firstborn of Israel and the Levites) were covered and paid for. And in this process it exemplifies the bigger picture showing that the plan of salvation of God does cover everyone including His son, Jesus, who actually paid the ultimate price for our sins. As God created and originally accepted His creation (which entered into sin, as illustrated by the Israelites going into Egypt), God also accepted His Son for the redemption of His creation. Again, to illustrate this from the mind and mouth of God to the ears and mind of man, much has to be done and explained. This is pretty deep "stuff"!

In the book of Numbers, there are listed the *Ten* Commandments of God. They contain all that is necessary for physical life here on earth. However, there was no way that finite man could keep the laws of an infinite God. So God literally illustrated how he could take care of this by "covering" the sins of man, even as Adam and Eve tried to "cover" themselves in the Garden after they sinned.

The Ten Commandments were placed in a special box or carrying container called the Arc of the Covenant. But the top of the Arc of the Covenant (in which the Ten Commandments were kept) was covered by a special top or covering called the Mercy Seat, telling that is was because of the mercy of God that man's sins can be covered (and eventually totally removed). It was made of gold and had the images of two winged heavenly creatures called cherubim facing each other. The Arc of the Covenant was so special that it was placed in the Holy of Holies, a most holy place of the temple separated from the people by a large veil or curtain. Only the High Priest could enter this Holy of Holies and only on the special Day of Atonement. But at the exact moment of the death of Jesus at the crucifixion, this veil or curtain was torn from top to bottom, illustrating that the sins of man were totally removed. Although mankind cannot keep them, God still has a way to cover them.

In the story where the Israelites arrived at the "Promised Land" (Canaan), there were twelve spies sent in to give a report on the land. However, *ten* of the twelve spies gave a bad report. "And they gave the children of Israel a bad report of the land they had spied out" (Numbers 13:32). Why would there be a story where ten of twelve spies would lament against going into the "Promised Land"? So God's orderly plan was that these spies (and those who followed their report) would not enter the Promised Land. However, God allowed the two who believed in Him would indeed enter in. Thus, within the plan of salvation, although there will be those who will not believe (and thus not "enter in"), God will let those who believe "enter in". This could be considered the main message of the Scripture. Sin brings destruction but God brings life. It is God's divine plan to dispense justice (and destruction) but it is also His plan to bring salvation. Contrasting these is important. Certainly this concept must be told in the Scripture.

Noah is listed as the *tenth* generation from God, not the third, not the seventh or any other number (Genesis 5:1-29). Although there was sin, which was worthy of destruction, God had a way for salvation and deliverance. Because of God's divine order and planning, destruction did take place, but so did deliverance.

There is the *tithe* or one *tenth (*Leviticus 27:30). Its purpose is to recognize the wholeness or completeness of God, and His divine and orderly plan, of which we are a part.

As the twelve tribes of Israel established themselves in the Promised Land, it was not a "coincidence" that *ten* would rebel and would be completely destroyed by Assyria in 621 B.C. But the other two tribes (Judah and Benjamin) would continue within God's orderly plan. The birth of Jesus Himself would come from this lineage. "And he said to Jeroboam, Take for yourself *ten* pieces: for thus says the Lord, the God of Israel, Behold, I will tear the kingdom out of the hand of Solomon and will give ten tribes to you" (1 Kings 11:31). "For the children of Israel walked in all the sins of Jeroboam which he did; they did not depart from them; until the Lord removed Israel out of his sight, as he had said by his servants the prophets. So Israel was carried away from their own land to Assyria, as it is to this day" (2 Kings 17:22–3).

In the following story found in Daniel, there are *ten* kingdoms as symbolized by the *ten* toes on the feet of the image that opposed to God's kingdom, yet God is aware and will deal with it. Because of sin, there will certainly be destruction. But because of redemption as a result of God's divine and orderly plan, salvation will also occur because is it God that will deal with it and conquer.

> And whereas you saw the feet and toes, part of the potters' clay, and part of iron, the kingdom shall be divided; but there shall in it the strength of the iron, for a much as you saw the

> iron mixed with miry clay. And the toes of the feet were part of iron, and part of clay, so the kingdom shall be partly strong and partly broken. And whereas you saw iron mixed with miry clay, they shall mingle themselves with the seed of men: but they shall not cleave one to another, even as iron is not mixed with clay. And in the days of these kings shall the God of heaven set up a kingdom, which shall never be destroyed: and the kingdom shall be left to other people, but it shall break in pieces and consume all these kingdoms, and it shall stand forever. (Daniel 2:41–4)

> And the *ten* horns out of this kingdom are the ten kings that shall arise: and another shall rise after them; and he shall be different from the first, and he shall subdue three kings ... But the judgment shall sit, and they shall take away his dominion, to consume and destroy it unto the end. And the kingdom and dominion, and the greatness of the kingdom under the whole heaven, shall be given to the people of the saints of the most High, whose kingdom is an everlasting kingdom, and all powers shall serve and obey him. (Daniel 7:24, 26–7)

At the end of time this divine and orderly plan will culminate in a final conclusion. Again there will be those who will be "destroyed", including Satan himself, and there will be those who will be "saved".

> And I stood upon the sand of the sea and saw a beast rise up out of the sea, having seven heads and *ten* horns, and upon the horns *ten* crowns, and upon his heads the name of blasphemy ... So he carried me away in the spirit into the wilderness: and I saw a woman sit upon a scarlet-colored beast, full of names of blasphemy, having seven heads and *ten* horns ... And the *ten* horns which you saw are ten kings, which have received no kingdom as yet; but receive power as kings one hour with the beast. These have one mind and shall give their power to the beast. These shall make way with the lamb (Jesus), and the lamb (Jesus) shall overcome them: for he is the Lord of lords,

> and King of kings and they that are with him are called, and chosen, and faithful ... and I saw the beast and the kings of the earth, and their armies, gathered together to make war against him that sat on the horse (Jesus), and against his army. And the beast was taken, and with him the false prophet that wrought miracles before him, which had received the mark of the beast (666), and them that worshiped his image. These both were cast alive into a lake of fire burning with brimstone. And the remnant were slain with the sword of him that sat upon the horse (Jesus). (Revelation 13:1; 17:3, 12; 19:19–20)

Nothing just happens. Although we can debate if something is the will of God, in His infinite wisdom, God knows of things that happen ... and of things that will happen. Certainly, without this attribute of God, there is no point for discussion anyway. "For we know that all things work together for good to them that love God, to them that are called according to his purpose" (Romans 8:28).

Other examples of the number *ten* include the following:

Fire came down from heaven *ten* times.

1. On Sodom and Gomorrah and surrounding cities (Genesis 19:24)
2. On the first offerings (Leviticus 9:24)
3. On Nadab and Abihu (Leviticus 10:2)
4. On the murmurers at Taberah (Numbers 11:1)
5. On Korah and his company (Numbers 16:35)
6. On Elijah's offering at Mt. Carmel (1 Kings 18:38)
7. On Elijah's enemies (2 Kings 1:10)
8. Again on Elijah's enemies (2 Kings 1:12)
9. On David's sacrifice (1 Chronicles 21:26)
10. On Solomon's sacrifice (2 Chronicles 7:1)

The people *rejoiced and shouted* for joy *ten* times.

1. When the fire from heaven consumed the Hebrew's sacrifices (Leviticus 9:24)
2. When the Israelites defeated of Jericho (Joshua 6:20)
3. When the Ark of the Covenant was brought into the camp (1 Samuel 4:5)
4. When Saul was chosen king of Israel (1 Samuel 10:24)
5. When Israel went to fight the Philistines (1 Samuel 17:20)
6. When Israel pursued the Philistines (1 Samuel 17:52)
7. When the Ark of the Covenant was brought back from the house Obed-edom (2 Samuel 6:15)
8. When God smote Jeroboam before Abijah (2 Chronicles 13:15)
9. When King Asa and the people heard Oded's prophecy (2 Chronicles 15:14)
10. When the foundation of the second Temple was laid (Ezra 3:11)

"He that covers his sin shall not prosper, but whoso confesses and forsakes them shall have mercy" (Proverbs 28:13). "That if you will confess with your mouth the Lord Jesus, and shall believe in your heart that God has raised him from the dead, you shall be saved" (Romans 10:9). Therefore, it was not a coincidence that there were *ten* persons who uttered confessions and acknowledged their sins. In addition, it is interesting that six of these were individuals (the number of man) and four (the number of fullness of the earth) were "we," as represented on behalf of an earthly nation. These include the following:

1. Pharaoh (Exodus 10:16)
2. Balaam (Numbers 22:34)
3. Achan (Joshua 7:20)
4. Saul (1 Samuel 26:21)

5. David (1 Chronicles 21:8)
6. Shimei (2 Samuel 19:20)
7. Hezekiah (2 Kings 18:14)
8. Nehemiah (Nehemiah 1:6)
9. Job (Job 7:20)
10. Micah (Micah 7:9)

The number *ten* represents the cycle of creation, ranging from the original perfection and fall of man through sin to the restoration and redemption through Jesus. "An Ammonite or a Moabite shall not enter the congregation of the Lord: even to their *tenth* generation shall they not enter the congregation of the Lord forever" (Deuteronomy 23:3). Once again, it is interesting to note that Ruth was a Moabitess that married Boaz and became great-grandmother of David, through whose lineage Jesus, the Redeemer would come.

There are *ten* "I am's" of Jesus written of in the book of John. These are the following:

1. I am the bread of life (6:35).
2. I am the bread of life which came down from heaven (6:41).
3. I am the living Bread (6:51).
4. I am the light of the world (8:12).
5. I am the one that bears witness of myself (8:18).
6. I am the door of the sheep (10:7).
7. I am the good shepherd (10:14).
8. I am the resurrection and the life (14:6).
9. I am the way, the truth, and the life (14:6).
10. I am the true vine (15:1).

Then of course there are the Ten Commandments themselves (Exodus 20:1-17). In a recent court case (ACLU v. Giles County Virginia School District) the Giles County School District was forced to remove the display of the Ten Commandments from a school[1]. In an attempt to compromise during mediation, the presiding judge suggested that the number of commandments be reduced to six, removing the first four that have the name of "God" in it [2, 3]. Of course that did not work out.

The fact there are *ten* commandments (not six) is just as important as the commandments themselves. Of course the number *ten* represents the divine order by God incorporated into His creation, including the pan of salvation. There need to be no more or no less than *ten*. The first four are laws concerning man's relationship with God, and the final six are laws concerning man's relationship with man.

The very first of the commandments is, "You shall have no other gods before me" (Exodus 20:1). Only when God is revered can man understand the remaining commandments. Man cannot violate commandments 2-10 without actually violating commandment number one. Thus it is the entire context that is truly needed. It is the entire Bible that is needed. There is indeed a divine order that is evident and the number *ten* exemplifies this.

The Number Eleven (11)

The number eleven is used in Scripture to signify a state of disorder, a state in which there is obvious incompletion, a state that needs some type of organization. A good example of this can be found toward the end of the life of the southern kingdom of Judah in 2 Chronicles 36.

> Jehoahaz was twenty and three years old when he began to reign and he reigned three months in Jerusalem. (Note the number three months that illustrates part of God's perfect plan.) And the king of Egypt put him down at Jerusalem and condemned the land in a hundred talents of silver and gold. And the king of Egypt made Eliakim his brother king over

> Judah and Jerusalem, and turned his name to Jehoiakim ... Jehiokim was twenty and five years old when he began to reign and he reigned *eleven* years in Jerusalem: and he did that which was evil in the sight of the Lord. Against him came up Nebuchadnezzar king of Babylon to bound him in fetters and to carry him to Babylon ... and Jehoiachin his son reigned in his stead. Jehoiachin was eight years old when he began to reign and he reigned three months and ten days (note the number three and ten as in God's perfect plan and divine order) in Jerusalem: and he did that which was evil in the sight of the Lord. And when the year was expired, King Nebuchadnezzar sent and brought him to Babylon ... and made Zedekiah his brother king over Judah and Jerusalem. Zedekiah was one and twenty years old when he began to reign and reigned *eleven* years. And he did that which was evil in the sight of the lord and humbled himself not before Jeremiah the prophet speaking from the mouth of the Lord.

Jehoikim, Jehoichin and Zedekiah were Judah's last three kings. During the reigns of these three kings there was tremendous unrest and turmoil in the kingdom of Judah, thus mentioning *eleven* year reigns of Jehiokim and Zedekiah. In 587 BC, Nebuchadnezzar, king of Babylon, completed his conquest of Judah, and most of the remaining people were carried into captivity. Scripture records that Zedekiah, the final king of Judah, reigned *eleven* years. It is understood that leadership should bring organization and security. It was during these disorganized and disarrayed reigns that complete dissolution of the kingdom of Judah took place. As part of the total scenario of the Bible, those that are incomplete, disorganized in disarray cannot survive. God is complete and divinely organized His creation.

Other examples of *eleven* include the following:

- *Eleven* dukes of Edom (Genesis 36:40–43 and 1 Chronicles 1:51–4): Edom is another name for Esau, twin brother to Jacob. Jacob had twelve sons. The organization as governed by God among the tribes of Jacob (who became Israel) is unmatched.

There was an unmatched hatred among the Edomites and Israelites. There was a lack of organization and a state of incompleteness of the *eleven* dukes of Edom.

- *Eleven* days from Horeb to Kadesh Barnea (Deuteronomy 1:2–3): What should have taken *eleven* days to travel took the Israelites forty years to travel. Although God did lead and guide, the Israelites had rebelled against God at Kadesh Barnea. And as a result, they were essentially in a state of disarray. They were imperfect and disorganized. With the exception of Joshua and Caleb, they disintegrated in the desert. It is interesting that it was in the *eleventh* month of the fortieth year that Moses addressed the Israelites concerning the incident.

- *Eleven* sons of Jacob (Genesis 32:22–33:28): This scripture is explicit in mentioning that at this time, Jacob only had *eleven* sons. At this time, Jacob wrestled with an angel under the name of Jacob. It was a time of incompleteness and disorganization of the not yet completed nation of Israel. However, after this encounter with God, Jacob's name was changed to Israel (prince) and his twelfth son, Benjamin, would be born later, completing the organization of the twelve tribes of Israel.

Of course, Jacob (Israel) had twelve sons. Joseph, the firstborn of Jacob's first love, Rachel, was sold by his own brothers into slavery and wound up in Egypt, thus leaving behind *eleven*. During this time (when there were only the *eleven* sons living together as family), they were disorganized and in disarray. They eventually had to travel to Egypt in order to survive, and they were saved by their brother, Joseph.

Eleven kings and rulers mentioned that they were offended by being told the truth. These include the following:

1. Pharaoh (Exodus 10:28)

2. Balak (Numbers 24:10)

3. Jeroboam (1 Kings 13:4)

4. Ahab (1 Kings 22:27)

5. Naaman (2 Kings 5:12)

6. Asa (2 Chronicles 16:10)

7. Joash (2 Chronicles 24:21)

8. Uzziah (2 Chronicles 26:19)

9. Jehoiakim (Jeremiah 26:21)

10. Zedekiah (Jeremiah 32:3)

11. Herod (Matthew 14:3)

Jesus spoke on the truth. "I am ... the truth" (John 14:6). People who do not believe the truth or desire to even know the truth will wind up in a state of disorganization and disarray.

The Number Twelve (12)

Of course the number twelve is a product of 3 x 4. Thus, the divine perfection of number three once factored into the physical world would equal perfection in physical governmental. This can be readily seen in the *twelve* tribes of Israel and the *twelve* disciples of Jesus. The number *twelve* is found 187 times in the Bible, twenty-two times in the book of Revelation.

In addition to the *twelve* tribes of Israel, Aaron's rod blossomed and gave *twelve* branches, representing the twelve tribes (Numbers 17).

There were *twelve* individuals who are named in the Bible as people who have been anointed. In order, these are the following:

1–5. Aaron and his four sons (Exodus 29:7–9)

6. Saul (1 Samuel 10:1)

7. David, the first time (1 Samuel 16:13)

8. Absalom (2 Samuel 19:10)

9. Solomon (1 Kings 1:39)

10. Jehu (2 Kings 9:6)

11. Joash (2 Kings 11:12)

12. Jehoahaz (2 Kings 23:30)

Even within the order of these listed, it is interesting to note that following a priestly foundation, Saul was the first anointed, but he was the people's choice. David, God's choice, was the seventh anointed. And although Solomon was wise, he was the ninth (finality, judgment) anointed. His was the last kingship of a unified Israel. The northern kingdom of Israel was utterly destroyed in 721 BC, and the southern kingdom of Judah was carried away to captivity by Babylon in 587 BC.

From the original twelve tribes of Israel through Jehoahaz and Zedekiah, the number twelve illustrates the physical establishment of human government and rule as purposed by God. Jehoahaz was the last king (number *twelve*) spoken of as being anointed. He ruled for only three months as he was the fourth king from the end of the kingdom of Judah. And as previously mentioned, Jehoiakim (Josiah's second son) ruled for eleven years. Jehoiakim's son, Jehoichin, then ruled three months. Zedekiah (Josiah's third son) was the last king and ruled eleven years, too. At this point in time and history, there was considerable disorganization, and the state of Judah was in disarray, and marked the end of Judah. Note how even all of these numbers work together. It shows how wrong things can be (physically) and events that can lead to good and bad results. In an attempt to describe the divine perfection that is found in God, God utilized the physical or human governmental array to illustrate and enhance the understanding of His Word.

In addition to Old Testament accounts, the use of *twelve* is used in the New Testament. Jesus was fully God (spiritual) but He was also fully man (physical). Aside from the announcement of His birth (Christmas), his first public appearance happened when He was *twelve* years old (Luke 2:42). At His trial prior to His crucifixion, Jesus mentioned *twelve* legions of angels could be summoned (Matthew 26:53).

Within the walls of Jerusalem, there were twelve gates. These include the following:

1. The Sheep Gate (Nehemiah 3:1)
2. The Fish Gate (Nehemiah 3:3)
3. The Old Gate (Nehemiah 3:6)
4. The Valley Gate Nehemiah 3:13)
5. The Dung Gate (Nehemiah 3:13)
6. The Fountain Gate (Nehemiah 3:15)
7. The Water Gate (Nehemiah3:26)
8. The Horse Gate (Nehemiah 3:28)
9. The East Gate (Nehemiah 3:29)
10. The Miphkad Gate (Nehemiah 3:31)
11. The Ephraim Gate (2 Chronicles 25:23)
12. The Prison Gate (Nehemiah 12:39)

Of course, each of these is a sermon in and of itself. And the New Jerusalem will have *twelve* foundations of precious stones, *twelve* gates of pearl, *twelve* angels, and the *twelve* names of Israel at the gates. By combining Old and New Testament illustrations of the number *twelve*, other instances where the number twelve appears include the following:

- The *twelve* stones of the altar of the alliance (Exodus 24:4)
- The *twelve* names engraved on the pectoral (Exodus 28:21)
- The *twelve* loaves of permanent offering on the golden table (Leviticus 24:5)

- The *twelve* branches to confirm the choice of Aaron (Numbers 17:2)
- The *twelve* explorers sent in Canaan (Deuteronomy 1:23)
- The *twelve* stones chosen by the *twelve* men in the Jordan to make a monument (Joshua 4:3)
- The *twelve* administrators of Solomon for all Israel (1 Kings 4:7)
- The *twelve* oxen of the bronze sea (1 Kings 7:25)
- The *twelve* strips made with the cloak of Ahijah (1 Kings 11:30)
- The *twelve* stones of the altar of Elijah (1 Kings 18:31)
- The sacrifices of the *twelve* animals (Numbers 7:87 and 29:17)
- The three series of *twelve* silver bowls offered for the dedication of the altar (Numbers 7:84)
- The *twelve* curses proclaimed by Moses to all men of Israel (Deuteronomy 27:15–26)
- The *twelve* springs of Elim (Exodus 15:27)
- The *twelve* tributes of Israel: Judah, Reuben, Gad, Asher, Naphtali, Manasseh, Simeon, Levi, Issachar, Zebulun, Joseph, and Benjamin (Revelation 7:5–8)

God is spirit and man is physical. But God created us in the physical state. Understanding the spiritual with a physical mind can be difficult. Although the organizational view of this spiritual, complete, organized God can be spoken of, it is only when it is placed in the context of the physical that man can better understand it. Thus, the organization of man as illustrated in structured government can be used to more fully illustrate the spiritual nature of God.

The Number Thirteen (13)

The number *thirteen* has long been associated with superstition and darkness. Some have postulated that the origin of the number *thirteen* as a bad number is associated with the Last Supper of Christ. Counting Jesus and His twelve disciples, there were *thirteen* in attendance. And of course, Jesus was crucified and in the grave within twenty-four hours. Hence, there is the expression, "Friday the *thirteenth*."

However, when examining the biblical accounts of the number *thirteen*, we find that *thirteen* is generally associated with rebellion, apostasy, rejection, or general enemies of God. It usually involves time and space. For example, consider Genesis 14:1–4:

> And it came to pass in the days of Amraphel king of Shinar, Arioch king of Ellasar, Chedorlaomer king of Elam and Tidal king of nations; That these made war with Birsha king of Gomorrah, Sinab king of Admah and Shemeber, king of Zeboim, and the king of Bela, which id Zoar. All these joined together in the vale of Siddim, which is the salt sea. Twelve years they served Chedorlaomer, and in the *thirteenth* year they rebelled.

Those who rebelled were later defeated in battle. Nimrod, the chief rebel after the Flood, was the *thirteenth* generation in the line of Ham. In a more poignant story, Haman, a chief minister of King Ahasuerus of Persia, sought to destroy the Jews (God's chosen people).

> And Haman said unto the king Ahasuerus, There is a certain people scattered abroad and dispersed among the people in all the provinces of your kingdom; and their laws are diverse from all people; neither do they keep the king's laws; therefore it is not for the king's profit to allow them to continue. If it pleases the king, let it be written that they may be destroyed ... Then the king's scribes were called on the thirteenth day of the first month and there was written according to all that Haman had commanded. (Esther 3:8, 12)

But Esther, the queen, told her husband, the king, of the plot.

> Then Esther the queen answered and said, If I have found favor in your sight, O king, and if it please the king, let my people at my request: For we are sold, I and my people, to be destroyed, to be slain, and to perish. But if we had been sold for bondmen and bondwomen, I held my tongue, although the enemy could not have compensated for the king's damage. Then the king Ahasuerus answered and said unto Ester the queen, Who is he, and where is he, that dares presume in his heart to do so. And Esther said, The adversary and enemy is wicked Haman ... So they hanged Haman on the gallows that he had prepared for Mordecai. (Esther 7:3–6, 10)

The Jews were authorized to protect themselves and destroy their enemy.

> Wherein the king granted the Jews which were in every city to gather themselves together, and to stand for their life, to destroy, to slay, and to cause to perish, all the power of the people and province that would assault them, both little ones and women, and to take the spoil of them for a prey. Upon one day in all the provinces of king Ahasuerus, on the *thirteenth* day of the twelfth month, which is the month Adar. (Esther 8:11–12)

Those who opposed the Jews were destroyed. Thus, the enemies of God and His people can be expressed in the number *thirteen.* All of the gematria names (Hebrew and Greek) of Satan are divisible by *thirteen.*

Other expressions of the number *thirteen* include the following:

> In Mark 7:20–23, Jesus mentions *thirteen* things that defile a person. "And he (Jesus) said, That which comes out of the man, that defiles the man. For from within, out of the heart of men, proceed—"

1. evil thoughts
2. adulteries
3. fornications
4. murders
5. thefts
6. covetousness
7. wickedness
8. deceit
9. lewdness
10. an evil eye
11. blasphemy
12. pride
13. foolishness

Thirteen famines are also recorded in the Scriptures.

1. Genesis 12:10
2. Genesis 26:1
3. Genesis 41:54
4. Ruth 1:1
5. 2 Samuel 21:1
6. 1 Kings 18:1
7. 2 Kings 4:38
8. 2 Kings 7:4

9. 2 Kings 25:3
10. Nehemiah 5:3
11. Jeremiah 14:1
12. Luke 15:14
13. Acts 11:28

The Number Fourteen (14)

The number fourteen is a multiple of seven, and thus, it can be described as a double portion of spiritual perfection. In addition, it can be used to illustrate deliverance and salvation, and thus, it can lead to victory.

Passover was initiated on the *fourteenth* day of the first month.

> And the Lord spake unto Moses and Aaron in the land of Egypt, saying, This month shall be to you the beginning of months, it shall be the first month of the year to you ... You lamb shall be without blemish of the first year: ... and you shall keep it until the *fourteenth* day of the same month: and the whole assembly of the congregation shall kill it in the evening ... it is the Lord's Passover. (Exodus 12:1–2, 5–6, 11)

This illustrated the deliverance of the Israelites from the Egyptians.

Thus, it is a kingly number as the Lord, the King of Kings, led His people out of Egypt and defeated Pharaoh's army. The gematria of King David's name is *fourteen*. From David to the captivity of Judah by the Babylonians was *fourteen* kings (generations), and from the captivity to Jesus was *fourteen* generations. "So all the generations from Abraham to David are *fourteen* generations; and from David until the carrying away into Babylon are *fourteen* generations; and from the carrying away into Babylon to Christ are *fourteen* generations" (Matthew 1:17).

Matthew did not just mention the genealogy of Jesus. Although Matthew did list the names included in Jesus' human ancestry, he specifically listed it from King David (not from Abraham or Adam as is listed in Luke 3:23-38). In addition, Matthew specifically mentioned the number *fourteen*. It is also interesting that is the Gospel of Matthew also records the Wise Men asking, "Where is he that is born king of the Jews" (Matthew 1:2). It would seem that Matthew's interest (in the writing of the book of Matthew) was on the kingship of Jesus.

The double portion of Jesus as being spiritual perfected as fully God yet fully man can best be described as that He is King of all Kings and Lord of all Lords. "And he (Jesus) has on his robe and on his thigh a name written, King of Kings and Lord of Lords" (Revelation 19:16). The number *fourteen* best describes this concept the Jesus is indeed King of Kings!

The Number Fifteen (15)

The number *fifteen* is also used in Scripture numerous times and in the same meaning. The number fifteen can be attained by multiplying the numbers three and five. Three represents the Trinity or the completeness and fullness of God. The number five represents the grace of God. Therefore, any number of fifteen refers to an act by God with His grace (or because of His Grace). "And the waters prevailed exceedingly upon the earth; and all the high hill, that were under the whole heaven, were covered. *Fifteen* cubits upward did the waters prevail; and the mountains were covered" (Genesis 7:19–20). God specifically sent the rain (Flood), but He also specifically saved Noah's family.

Following a moving prayer by King Hezekiah of Judah, God added fifteen years to his life. "And I will add *fifteen* years; and I will deliver you and this city out of the hand of the king of Assyria; and I will defend this city for my servant David's sake" (2 Kings 20:6). You should also consider the following that illustrate acts by God because of His Grace:

- In Exodus, the Hebrews left Egypt on the *fifteenth* day of the month (Numbers 33:3).
- In Leviticus, the Feast of the Unleavened Bread was on the *fifteenth* day of the fifth month (Leviticus 23:6).

- In Leviticus, the Feast of Tabernacles was on the *fifteenth* day of the seventh month (Leviticus 23:34).
- In Esther, the Jews celebrated the deliverance from Mordecai's devious plan called the feast or days of Purim on the fourteenth and fifteenth days of Adar (Esther 9:18-32).
- In Acts, during a storm, Paul's ship was anchored safely off shore in fifteen fathoms of water (Acts 27:13-28).

To be sure, any act by God toward His beloved creation is an act of grace and mercy. Judgment is deserved but mercy is given.

It is at the number *fifteen* that further mentioning of numeric illustrations in Scripture is not really necessary to emphasize the significance of numbers and unity of their use in the Bible. After all, the idea of Jesus as King and ultimate authority with an expressed purpose of Himself and His creation should suffice. Numbers of greater magnitude are certainly derived from smaller numbers that merely arranged in certain formats such as addition and multiplication. It should not be the task to examine all of numbers and employ the ways and means in which they can be derived. And surely any number in our numeric system can be derived in some way, and it is interesting that the Bible utilizes many numbers and their derivation. However, only a couple of other numeric expressions are needed of discussion within this text to illustrate the unity of the Bible. These numbers are 16, 17 in sequence and the numbers 40, 153 and 666.

The Number Sixteen (16)

The number *sixteen* in the Bible is another number that briefly "pops up". It seems to express God's steadfast love for His creation. For example in 1 Corinthians 13:4–8, the apostle Paul lists *sixteen* things about the quality of love (charity).

1. Love suffers long.
2. Love is kind.

3. Love does not envy.
4. Love does not parade itself.
5. Love is not puffed up.
6. Love does not behave rudely.
7. Love does not seek its own.
8. Love is not provoked.
9. Love thinks no evil.
10. Love does not rejoice in iniquity.
11. Love rejoices in the truth.
12. Love bears all things.
13. Love believes all things.
14. Love hopes all things.
15. Love endures all things.
16. Love never fails.

The Number Seventeen (17)

The final number to be included in sequence is the number *seventeen.* The number *seventeen* represents the perfection of spiritual order. It is the seventh prime number. It can be attained by 7 + 10 (adding perfect order with spiritual order) or 2 x 7 +3 (contrasting multiplied by spiritual perfection and adding the completeness and fullness of God). The entire Scripture (Old Testament and New Testament) had to be totally perfect in its completion. From Adam to Abraham, from Moses to the manger scene of Jesus' birth, from the crucifixion on Golgotha and the beginning of the church to the book of Revelation, all had to be done for the completeness of spiritual order. It represents vanquishing the Enemy (ultimately Satan). Thus, it can also represent immortality.

This is not just an exercise of adding numbers to get a number. The number seventeen is actually written in Scripture as a number *seventeen* but it is also shown as derivatives of other numbers, as well. Blessings of the New Testament are shown to be more highly emphasized than those of the Old Testament, both in number and in importance. Old Testament concepts were spiritual (the number seven), but the New Testament is a testament of grace (the number five), or rather a double portion of grace (5 x 2 = 10).

The number *seventeen* is obtained by adding seven and ten. In the Old Testament, the Day of Atonement came on the tenth day of the seventh month (Leviticus 23:27). Of course, the atonement means victory over death. In the New Testament, he beast of Revelation had seven heads and ten horns (Revelation 13:1), and of course, this beast was defeated in the end.

The number *seventeen* is listed as a word of its own (*seventeen*) and has been shown as components of the number *seventeen* (7 + 10). Therefore, it seems to be an important numeric expression on its own. For example, the Flood began on the *seventeenth* day of the second month (Genesis 7:11), and the Ark came to rest on Mt. Ararat on the *seventeenth* day of the seventh month (Genesis 8:4).Joseph was sold into slavery at the age of *seventeen* (Genesis 37:2). Jacob lived in Egypt for *seventeen* years (Genesis 47:28). Of course, when the Israelites "came out of Egypt," they symbolically "came out of sin" by redemption as the Passover was instituted.

The number *seventeen* is illustrated into the age the patriarchs of Abram (Abraham), Isaac, and Jacob (Israel) died. Abraham died at age 175, Isaac at 180, and Jacob at 147.

- Abraham: 175 = 5 x 5 x 7 and 5 + 5+ 7 = 17
- Isaac: 180 = 6 x 6 x 5 and 6 + 6 + 5 = 17
- Jacob: 147 = 7 x 7 x 3 and 7 + 7+ 3 = 17

Note how the progression proceeds with the number five (grace) and the number seven (perfection) for Abraham. However, the number five (grace) and the number six (imperfection) are seen for

Isaac, and the number seven (perfection) followed by the number three for the Trinity or completeness of God is present for Jacob (Israel).

The number *seventeen* is represented at Pentecost, not only naming the Galileans but citing sixteen other national groups (Acts 2:7–11)

In the book of Romans, Paul lists seven things that may split our relationship with God, but then lists ten answers in response.

> Who shall separate us from the love of Christ? Shall tribulation, or distress, or persecution, or famine, or nakedness, or peril, or sword? As it is written, For your sake we are killed all the day long; we are accounted as sheep for the slaughter. Nay, in all these things we are more than conquers through him that loved us. For I am persuaded, that neither death, nor life, nor angels, nor principalities, nor powers, nor things present, nor things to come, nor height, nor depth, nor any other creature, shall be able to separate us from the love of God, which is in Christ Jesus our Lord. (Romans 8:36–9)

The following is said to separate us from God.

1. Tribulation
2. Distress
3. Persecution
4. Famine
5. Nakedness
6. Peril
7. Sword

The following illustrates God's response of those that cannot separate us from Him.

1. Death
2. Life
3. Angels
4. Principalities
5. Powers
6. Present things
7. Future things
8. Height things
9. Deep things
10. Any thing (creature)

As can be seen from numbers higher than eleven, spiritual meanings can be taken from the ways and means in which these higher numbers can be derived from lower numbers. It is interesting how the Bible is able to accomplish this and utilize it with unity from the Old Testament through the New Testament.

It's also an important factor in the number 153, which we will discuss later.

The Number Forty (40)

A number that is can easily be recognized in Scripture is the number *forty* and therefore, cannot be left out. The number *forty* can be shown to be a product of five (grace) and eight (renewal or new beginning). It could also be shown to be a product of four (divine perfection in God's physical creation) and ten divine order of God's creation and purpose). It is mentioned 146 times in the Bible. It represents a period of time of trials or testing, which is followed by something else. The first mention of the number *forty* is in Genesis 7. "And the rain was upon the earth *forty* days and *forty* nights ... And the flood was *forty* days upon the earth" (Genesis 7:12, 17). It rained *forty* days, and following the rain was a great flood! There was a great flood, and great destruction followed! But a new beginning followed that.

Moses' life can be divided into three forty-year segments. He lived *forty* years in Egypt under the watch of the queen and Pharaoh, learning to be royalty. He was found by Pharaoh's daughter and during this time he lived inside the walls of the Egyptian king as part of the royal family. In spite of his high position in Egyptian royalty, Moses was forced to flee Egypt and live in the desert in an area called Midian. That was followed by another *forty* year period of living in the desert of Midian, learning to be nobody. As a herdsman he lived a simple life, far different from his Egyptian home life. But it was here that Moses literally met God at the "burning bush" and was instructed by God that it would be he who would lead the Hebrews from the slavery of Egypt (Exodus 3:1-8) .

He returned to Egypt and led the children of Israel out of Egypt and in the wilderness toward the Promised Land (Canaan) for his final *forty* year period. It was during this forty year period of "wanderings" that the Ten Commandments and the laws were given, as well as stories of commitment, grace and judgment. That, of course, was followed by the Israelites eventually settling in Canaan. Of course the history of the development of Israel as a nation soon followed.

While Moses was getting the Ten Commandments, he was in the mountain for *forty* days. And of course, when he came down, God's law physically written down, there followed the period of the law. "And Moses went into the midst of the cloud, and got up into the mount: and Moses was in the mount *forty* days and *forty* nights" (Exodus 24:18).

Even Jesus was in the wilderness, fasting for *forty* days, and that time was followed by temptations from Satan. "Then Jesus was led up by the Spirit into the wilderness to be tempted of the devil. And when he had fasted *forty* days and *forty* nights, he was afterward hungry. And when the devil came to him, he said, If you are the Son of God, command that these stones be made of bread" (Mathew 4:1–3). It was after this that the ministry of Jesus followed.

Whenever we are trying to learn something, it takes time. Oftentimes we have to learn the hard way by experiences, some of which may not be pleasant. So it is in Scripture. The individuals and the nations are given these examples by God, and they may need time to reflect, understand, and learn those things that are being taught. We, in turn, can read these Scripture examples and learn from them. The number *forty* may represent a time of trial or condition, but it is also followed by another time period. Other illustrations of *forty* include the following:

- Isaac was *forty* years old when he took Rebecca to be his wife (Genesis 25:20).
- The Israelite spies stayed in the land of Canaan for *forty* days (Numbers 13:25).
- Caleb was *forty* years old when Moses sent him into Canaan to spy. He and Joshua were the only spies who wanted to go into Canaan, but they were outvoted, resulting in *forty* years of wandering by the Israelites (Joshua 14:7 and Number 14:33).
- Othniel judged Israel for *forty* years (Judges 3:11).
- Barak judged Israel for *forty* years (Judges 5:31).
- Gideon judged Israel for *forty* years (Judges 8:28).
- Eli judged Israel *forty* years (1 Samuel 4:18).
- David ruled Israel for *forty* years (2 Samuel 5:5).
- Solomon ruled Israel for *forty* years (Chronicles 9:30).
- Jonah preached to the Assyrians for *forty* days (Jonah 3:4).
- Jehoash ruled Judah for *forty* years (2 Kings 12:2).
- Ezekiel lay on his right side for *forty* days to symbolize the *forty* years of Judah's transgressions before the Lord (Ezekiel 4:6).

It would seem dire that man needs so many examples to illustrate a point. But God is patient and even though most will not heed these examples, God does indeed give these examples, anyway.

The Number One Hundred and Fifty-Three (153)

One of the reasons numbers at least through the number 17 had to be examined is because of the number 153. It is only after we examine numbers through seventeen, that we can discuss the number *153*, which comes from John 21:11. As interesting as the number itself is, this is the only place in the Bible that the number *153* is written. "Simon Peter went up, and drew the net to land full of great fishes, a *hundred and fifty and three*." This is the number of fish caught by seven disciples following the resurrection of Jesus. The number *153* would not seem significant at all were it not for this scripture. Why could it have not been written, "A lot of fish?" Why a specific number and why this number? There have been many who have tried to explain the significance of this number, including things such as the number of species of fish in the Sea of Galilee. However, there seems to be more to it.

Jesus continues His teaching in this text by asking Peter three times if he loves Him. The message of John 21 is that Jesus did live, teaching us the way of the Father (of the Old Testament) and inciting us to go out and be fishers of men so that they, too, may know Him as the disciples do. Thus, all of the previously listed numbers in sequence (1-17) can be seen in the number *153*. It is the final outcome of all numbers (up to the number seventeen) and divisible by three. Thus, contained within any of these numbers is the number three. If the number three represents the completeness and fullness of God (the Trinity), then the fullness and completeness of God is within each of these numbers, illustrating the importance of one third. "And his tail drew the third part of the stars of heaven, and cast them to the earth: and the dragon stood before the woman which was ready to devour her child as soon as it was born" (Revelation 12:4).

Now, if we were to add the numbers one through seventeen (seventeen being the highest number we have illustrated in succession from the number one), we get the number *153*.

1+2+3+4+5+6+7+8+9+10+11+12+13+14+15+16+17 = *153*

In other words, all of the other numbers and their associated meanings can be summed up in the number 153. The divine nature and purpose of God can be expressed here. For example, recall that the number three represents the divine perfection of God in the nature of the Father, Son and Holy Spirit. Thus, if you were to combine the Only (one) God (Trinity – Three) and His grace (five) and use the mathematic analogy of cubing the numbers one, three, and five you get 153.

$$(1)^3 + (3)^3 + (5)^3 = 1 + 27 + 125 = 153$$

or another view is

$$(17)\ (3+3+3) = 153$$

where everything (numbers through 17) that has been included in Scripture describes the very nature of God (three).In math, an act of repeating an operation or process is called iteration. If we were to take the numbers one through seventeen that are divisible by three (that is the number 3, 6, 9, 12, 15), cube those numbers and then cube the digits of the sums, the mathematical iteration results are very interesting. The operation (iteration) goes like this.

$$3^3 = 27 \text{ ...and } 2^3 + 7^3 = 351 \text{ ...and } 3^3 + 5^3 + 1^3 = 153$$

In this example, only two iterations (the operation of cubing/adding) were needed to reach the number 153. The number three, representing the Trinity (completeness of God) and two characteristics, judgment and grace can be seen.

We could do this for all the numbers up to 17 divisible by three. However, for brevity, following the number three, the numbers six and nine will be used as examples.

Using the number six, the next number in our list divisible by three, the iteration is as follows:

$$6^3 = 216 \ldots 2^3 + 1^3 + 6^3 = 225 \ldots 2^3 + 2^3 + 5^3 = 141 \ldots 1^3 + 4^3 + 1^3 = 66 \ldots 6^3 + 6^3 = 432 \ldots 4^3 + 3^3 + 2^3 = 99 \ldots 9^3 + 9^3 = 1458 \ldots 1^3 + 4^3 + 5^3 + 8^3 = 707 \ldots 7^3 + 0^3 + 7^3 = 351 \ldots 3^3 + 5^3 + 1^3 = 153$$

Note that there are nine iterations (cubing/adding) to reach 153. The number six represents incompleteness, and the number nine represents judgment.

Using the number nine, the next number in our list divisible by three, the iteration is as follows:

$9^3 = 729$ ... $7^3 + 2^3 + 9^3 = 1080$ ... $1^3+0^3+8^3+0^3 = 513$ ... $5^3+1^3+3^3+=153$

Note that there are only three iterations (cubing/adding) needed to reach 153. Also interesting is that if you take the number three (the Trinity) and cube it (and get the number nine), you still only need three iterations to reach 153.

Performing these mathematical operations and observing the results can be interesting. And one can certainly speculate about the numeric meanings of these exercises. Many of these meanings can be seen in the Bible. The number 153 seems to culminate what the entire Bible is about, including digging deep with the Scripture and through the Power of the Holy Spirit letting the message be delivered specifically to those who believe. In the context of John 21, pass the message of God along. Tell others about sin, judgment, grace, redemption, salvation, Jesus... Man was the instrument for writing the Bible and man can be literally fishers of men.

Regardless of what number and its meanings and interpretations are being discussed, care needs to be taken with any allegorical interpretations of all numbers (found in Scripture) in order to illustrate points.

The Number Six Hundred and Sixty-Six (666)

The final numeric expression to be discussed is the number 666. The number *666* is mentioned in the book of Revelation and signifies a name. "Here is wisdom, Let him that has understanding count, the number of the beast: for it is the number of a man; and his number is Six hundred threescore and six" (Revelation 13:18). This beast is an enemy of God. In fact, anyone who is not *for* God is *against* Him. "He that is not with me is against me; and he that gathers not with me scatters" (Matthew 12:30).

There are three examples in the Bible that stand out as being against God or being the enemies of God. The first is Goliath, essentially his height and demeanor. Goliath was *six* cubits (and a span) tall. His spearhead weighed *six* hundred shekels, and he had *six* pieces of armor (1 Samuel 17:4–7). Note the number six being shown three times (666). It turned out that Goliath was not as big as God. His armor did not save him, and his spearhead did no harm (to his enemy).

In contrast, the Christian is arrayed or depicted differently from Goliath. "Stand, therefore, having your loins girded about with truth and having on the breastplate of righteousness; And your feet shod with the preparation of the gospel of peace; Above all, taking the shield of faith. Wherewith you shall be able to quench all the fiery darts of the wicked. And take the helmet of salvation, and the sword of the Spirit, which is the word of God" (Ephesians 6:14–16). The breastplate of righteousness (through faith) is of God and fully protects, and the Word of God (the Bible) will suffice for our weapon.

A second example of being against God or His enemy is Nebuchadnezzar. He set up an image of himself that was *six*ty cubits tall and *six* cubits wide and there were *six* musical instruments that sounded (to indicate the time to bow down and worship the image) (Daniel 3:1, 5). When Shadrach, Meshach, and Abednego would not worship the image, they were thrown into a fiery furnace. "Then Nebuchadnezzar the king was astonished, and rose up in haste and said to his counselors, Did we not cast three men bound into the midst of the fire? They answered and said unto the king, True O king. He answered and said, Lo, I see four men loose, walking in the midst of the fore and they have no hurt; and the form of the fourth is like the Son of God" (Daniel 3:24–5). Nebuchadnezzar had built an image of himself to be seen by men, but it was he who saw the Son of God.

The third example is the one mentioned in the book of Revelation, whose number is 666. The number six is the number of man … or the imperfection of man. The fact that there are three sixes in this number indicates just how incomplete man is in and of himself. In other words, man is completely incomplete in his sinful state and by himself. Just as it may be difficult to understand just how perfect "perfect" is, so it is with understanding how evil "evil" is. The number 666 is the ultimate opposite of God.

A spectrum is a continuous sequence or range of characteristics or conditions. The spectrum of visible colors includes red, orange, yellow, green, blue, and violet. They demonstrate a range, depicting not one but a range of visible colors. With God and Satan, there is no spectrum. God is in total authority. If not, then what percentage? Satan is totally evil, not just a part. The number 666 represents the total opposite of God.

In the number 666, the first six is connected with pride … or rather "me." Following this, there is the second six, which is represented in the idea "I am mighty. I am exalted." The third six concerns following that attitude and belief in the lifestyle. (This is what Satan originally did. He thought of himself and not of God. He exalted himself, and since then, he has sought to destroy and devour what he can.) Thus, the totality of this is an individual who is interested in himself only. Thus, he feels powerful. He feels above any other dominion or authority, and he sets out to show it. And because Satan did this, he is the enemy of God. "We wrestle not against flesh and blood, but against principalities, against powers, against rulers of the darkness of this world, against spiritual wickedness in high places" (Ephesians 6:12) He and all of those who are like him and follow him are the ultimate enemy of God.

Even the wise Solomon fell prey to this notion of "I am exalted." "Now the weight of gold that came to Solomon in one year was six hundred threescore and six talents of gold" (1 Kings 10:14). As wise and renowned as Solomon was, he was certainly not as worthy as who and what God was!

Care certainly needs to be taken when we are discussing any number with any meanings or connotation in the Bible. But other numbers can be meaningful as well. There is a story about a physician who felt led to travel to a country in Africa and deliver some drugs and supplies. He was compelled to help out in a local clinic for a few days. As he was traveling to the village, his party had to make camp for the evening. During the night, a group of would-be thieves gathered together to rob the group of their supplies and maybe even kill them. But they did not.

Upon arrival at the village, the leader of the would-be thieves boldly approached the doctor. "We were going to attack you last night and steal all of your supplies … and we would have too, had it not been for all of your security guards."

The doctor was perplexed. They had not had any security guards. The doctor replied, "How many soldiers did you see?"

The would-be thief replied, "We counted twenty-six. Too many last night, but there will be a next time," the man smugly said, trying to scare the doctor.

But the doctor was still mystified and bewildered. Without thinking of their safety, his party had set out without any form of safety or security. He returned to his home church and was giving a report, and the story of his security guards came up. A voice from the congregation asked the doctor if he remembered what day (night) that event had taken place. The doctor told him. The man replied that several of the men of the church had felt a need to pray for the doctor on that very same day. They gathered at the church to pray. The man asked for all the men who were part of that prayer group to stand up. One by one, the men began to stand until all were standing. There were twenty-six. God uses numbers.

CHAPTER 4

Genealogies of the Bible

The Significance of Biblical Family Lineages

Probably one the most intriguing but least understood parts of the Bible is the genealogy. Whereas other spiritual texts simply write of do's and don'ts of spirituality and earthly living, the Bible spends a lot of time and effort in listing, explaining, and otherwise developing the history of man (and of God's redemptive plan of salvation). There must be a reason for names and events occurring in the Bible. To be sure, the family names, history, and ethnic development span the entire Bible. As family names and genealogy listings emerge, it becomes apparent that the unraveling and development of lives, circumstances, and occurrences of the Bible have a definite direction ... and plan.

There is a story, one reputed to be a myth. There was a Scottish farmer who saved an English nobleman's son from drowning. In an act of gratitude, the nobleman wanted to reward the farmer, but the farmer would not accept any payment. However, the nobleman was insistent and went on to pay for the education for the Scottish farmer's son. The Scottish farmer's son went on to college and became a famous scientist, discovering the antibiotic penicillin. His name was

Alexander Fleming. The nobleman's son went on to become England's prime minister, Winston Churchill. One wonders how the future may have played out had this event not occurred.

Because God created the physical, there had to be some description of the physical, including man and his family. And because man sinned and God made His redemptive plan of salvation, there had to be that development, including the good and the bad, essentially the choices made by man and God. There had to be learning stories along the way, ones depicting the nature of man and God, stories that we would use to examine ourselves. And all of this had to be told through the lives of mankind. Thus, the history of mankind and the nature of God can be expressed through lineage and genealogy. Thus, it can illustrate unity of Scripture.

To be sure, there has and will continue to be discussions as to the genealogies specifically listed in the Bible. As biblical scholars attempt to grasp and put together time lines and history, some genealogic listings do not seem to add up. There appears to be gaps within particular lineages. But the Bible is not a mere history book, requiring times and events to exactly add up according to our human understanding. That is not the purpose of the Bible. However, upon closer inspection of the biblical genealogies as listed, certain patterns do emerge, and from these patterns, we can better understand that the Bible is fitly framed together.

The following chart illustrates genealogies as listed in the Bible. Using the superscripts, a general commentary and description pertaining to that part of the genealogy will follow.

Genealogy History of the Bible

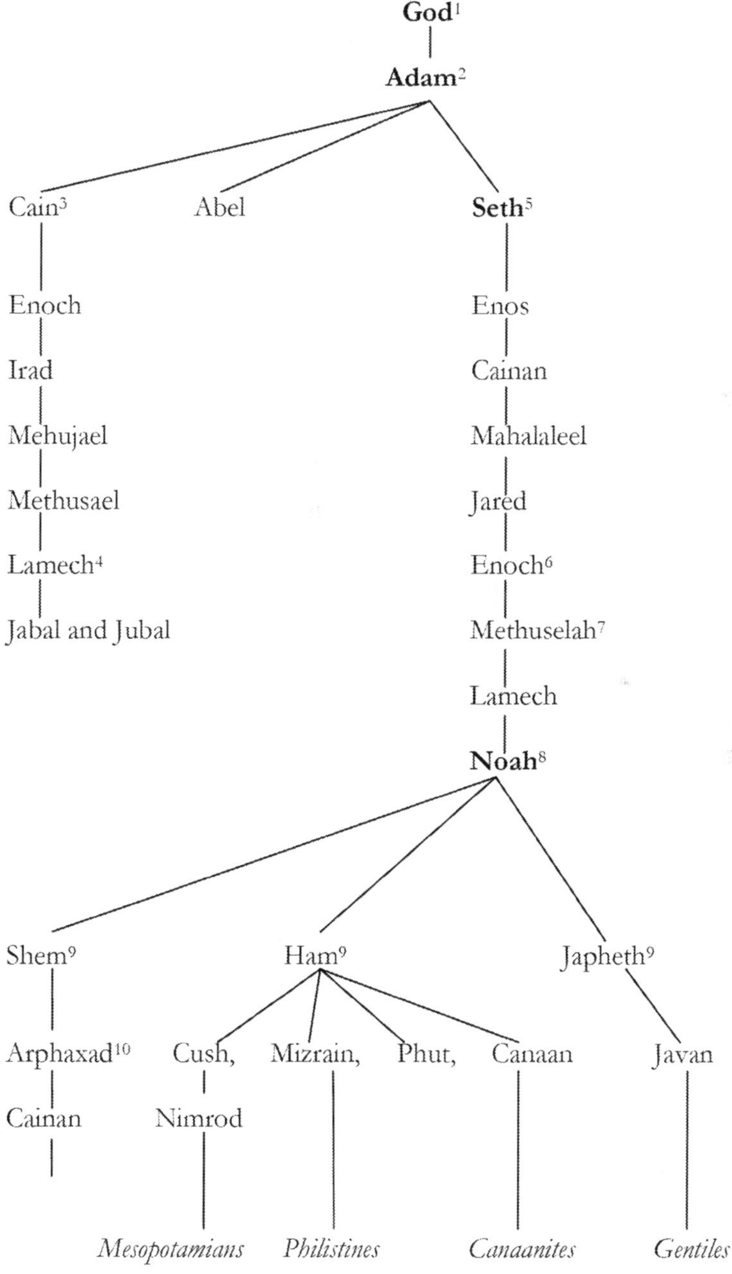

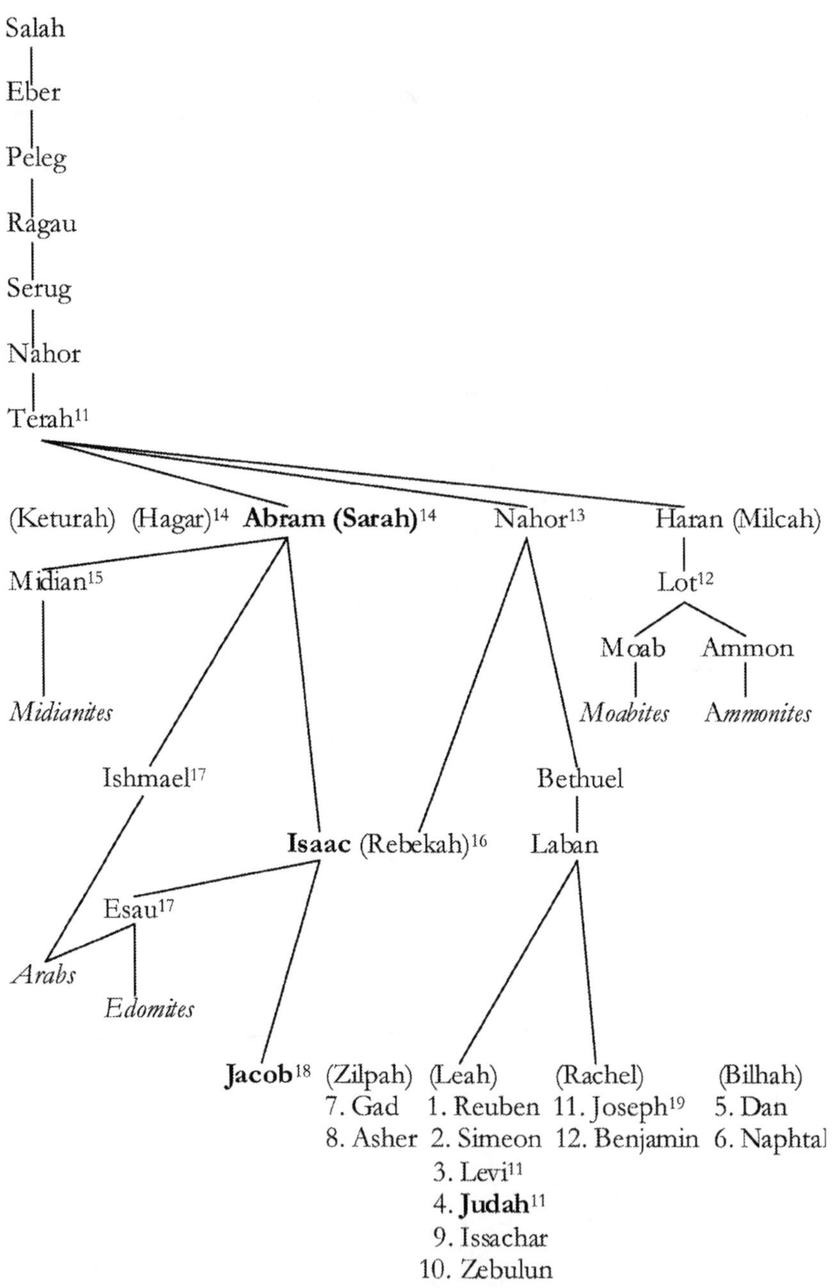

JEWS (Hebrews) The 12 Tribes of Israel [20]

Ephraim and Manasseh (sons of Joseph)[20]

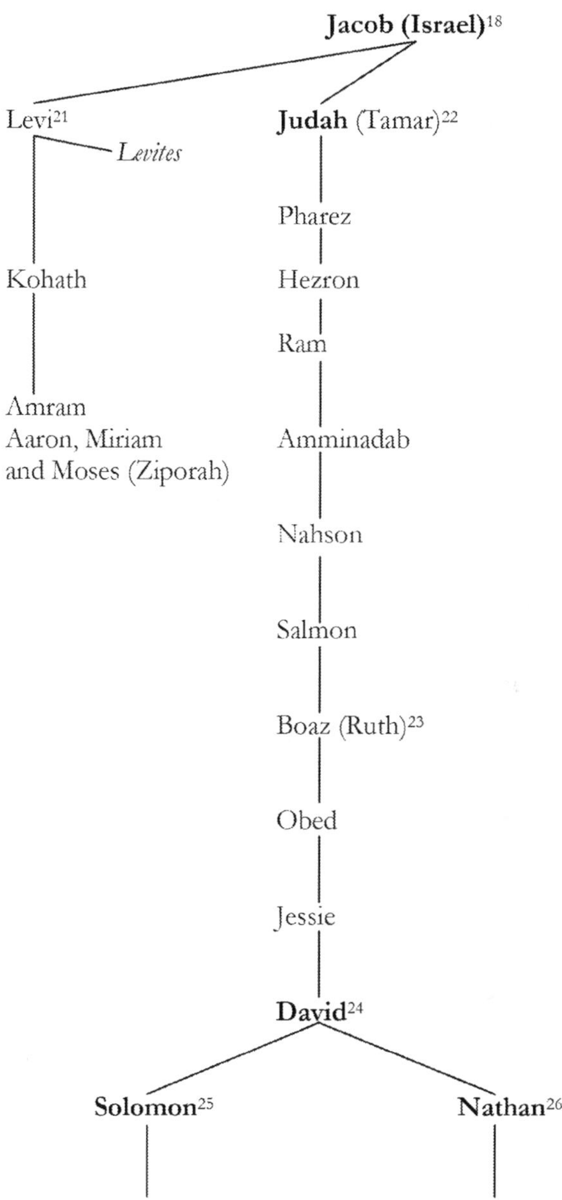
JEWS (Hebrews)
Jacob (Israel)[18]
Levi[21]
Levites
Judah (Tamar)[22]
Pharez
Hezron
Ram
Kohath
Amram
Aaron, Miriam
and Moses (Ziporah)
Amminadab
Nahson
Salmon
Boaz (Ruth)[23]
Obed
Jessie
David[24]
Solomon[25]
Nathan[26]

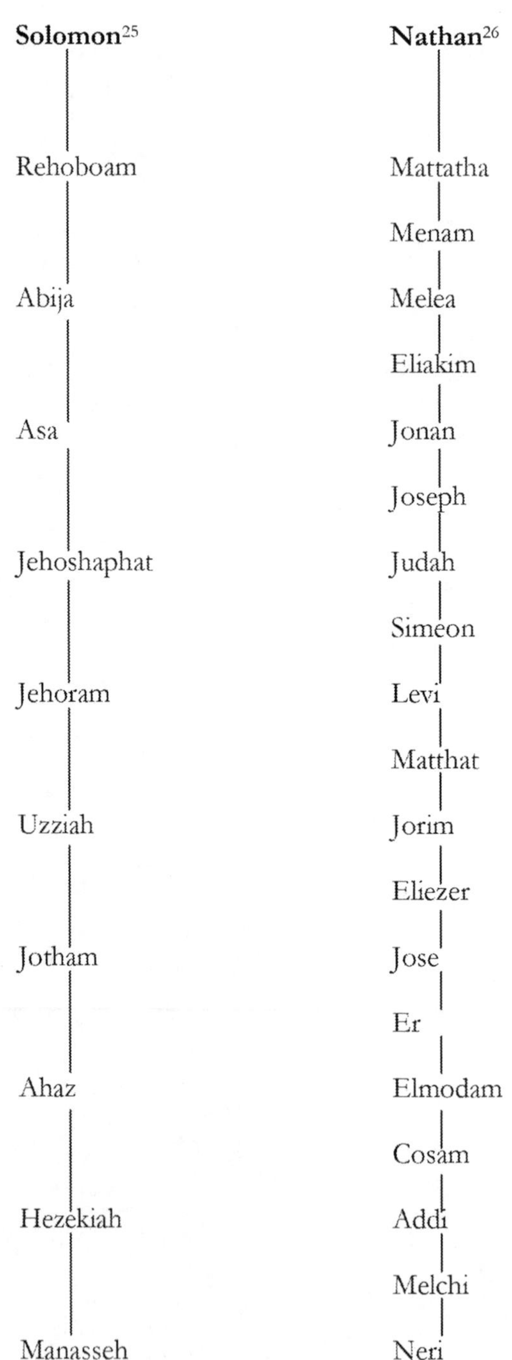

Solomon[25]
Rehoboam
Abija
Asa
Jehoshaphat
Jehoram
Uzziah
Jotham
Ahaz
Hezekiah
Manasseh
Nathan[26]
Mattatha
Menam
Melea
Eliakim
Jonan
Joseph
Judah
Simeon
Levi
Matthat
Jorim
Eliezer
Jose
Er
Elmodam
Cosam
Addi
Melchi
Neri

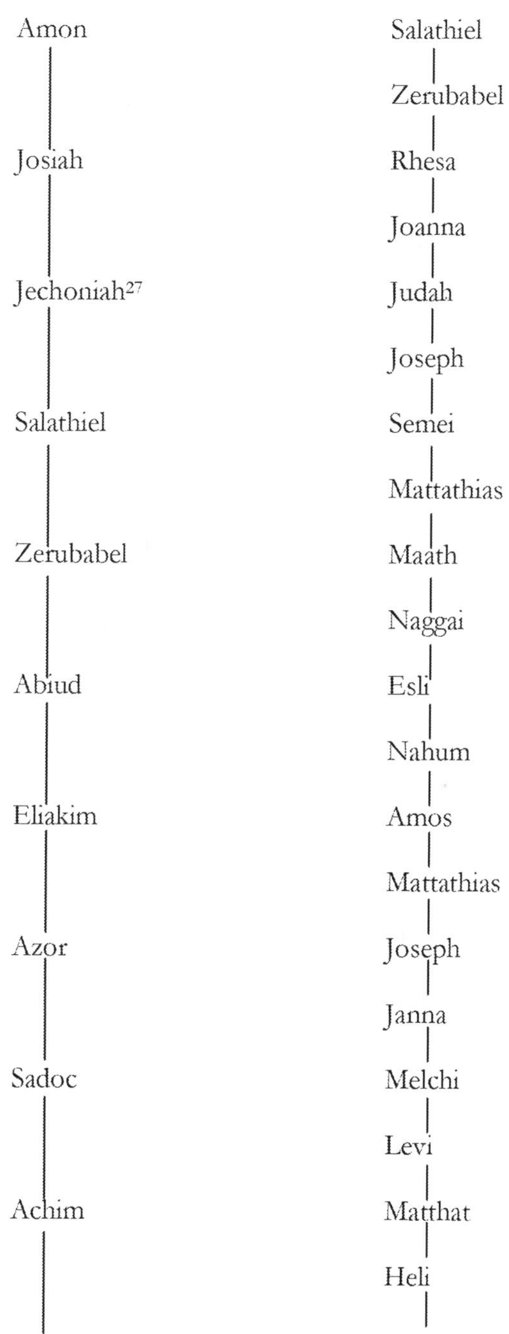
Amon
Josiah
Jechoniah[27]
Salathiel
Zerubabel
Abiud
Eliakim
Azor
Sadoc
Achim
Salathiel
Zerubabel
Rhesa
Joanna
Judah
Joseph
Semei
Mattathias
Maath
Naggai
Esli
Nahum
Amos
Mattathias
Joseph
Janna
Melchi
Levi
Matthat
Heli

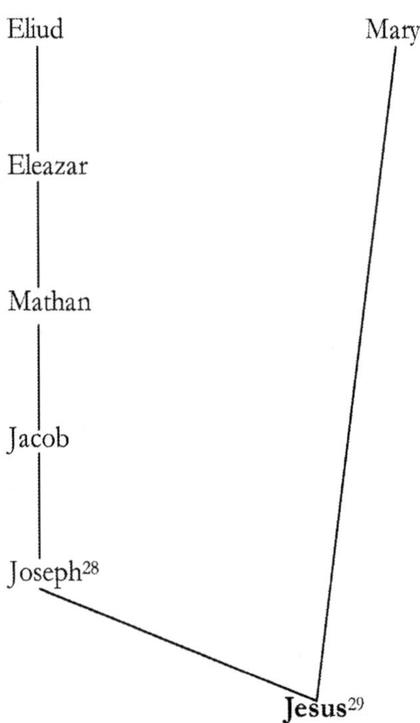
Eliud
Mary
Eleazar
Mathan
Jacob
Joseph[28]
Jesus[29]

[Notes 1 – 7]

This part of the genealogy establishes the creation of mankind, as purposed by God, the Creator. Through the lives and accounts of those listed we can begin to get the image and storyline of the concept of sin, result of sin and how mankind can recover and magnify God. The foundation of the Bible is established.

1 God, in His power and purpose created a physical world. To be sure, He also created the spiritual, including spiritual beings such as angels (Psalms 148:2-5), seraphim (Isaiah 6:1-10) and cherubim (Genesis 3:22-24, Ezekiel 1:1-14). Wanting to make His nature known, He created spiritual man and put him in a physical body. In His omnipotence and foreknowledge, He used the physical to bridge the spiritual and make known His nature.

Oftentimes questions occur as to how long a generation is or are all names of every generation are included in these listings. What is interesting however, are the names that are listed and number of generations shown. In studying the genealogies listed in the Bible, a relationship can be made with that of the numbers. To begin, in Genesis 2:10, there were *four* heads of a river listed in the Creation (indicating the physical), but only *one* river spoken of in Revelation 22:1 following the end of the physical time and space (indicating the spiritual).

2 Man was originally created holy and perfect, and he had a personal relationship with a holy and perfect God. But when man sinned, he lost that relationship. God (being holy) could not have a personal relationship with an unholy mankind. The "wages of sin is death" (Romans 6:23) and actually means separation from God. Adam (and Eve) knew their sin ... and nakedness. They tried to cover it up with fig leaves. This was unacceptable to God. God had to sacrifice a holy and perfect animal. Blood, therefore, was shed in order to cover up sin. This set in motion the sacrificial system acceptable to God, which eventually led to the sacrifice of Jesus. Jesus has been represented as the second Adam (Roman 5:12-14, 1 Corinthians 15:20-47). Through

one man, sin was introduced, and sin will be defeated through one man. "But the gift of God is eternal life through Jesus Christ our Lord" (Romans 6:23).

3 Cain, the first person born of the world, thought he could do something of his own accord to please God. He tried to offer to God something that he considered of his own doings. Of course, it was unacceptable to God. Abel, in his faith, offered a sacrifice that was pleasing to God. In Cain's envy and anger, he murdered his younger brother, Abel (Genesis 4:1-10).

Satan is the adversary of God (1 Peter 5:8, Job1:1-12). He tempted Eve and Adam and he tempted Cain. The first born killed the second born. Satan is certainly trying to sabotage and ruin God's creation. One could likely search the Scriptures and try to summarize and point out facts and actualities that would seem to fit a hypothesis or bias. After all, that is the nature of Satan. He disguises and deceives even God's Word for his own purpose. Satan is always willing to confuse and deceive those who are unwittingly willing to succumb to that temptation.

But Satan is limited (unlike God) and in his attempt to deceive and confuse mankind, Satan imitates God. There are only *six* generation listed from Cain, unlike the generations following Seth. Not only is the lineage limited in its listing, but names are similar to that of the lineage of Seth (Enoch, Lamech, Methusael/Methuselah). The events and accounts of the Bible as purposed by God, however, will pass through the lineage of Seth.

4 There are only *six* generations of Cain listed. Lamech is the *sixth* listed from Adam. He married two wives, and he was a murderer (Genesis 4:16-24). That which is unholy means death, life that was taken away. Adam sinned. His firstborn, Cain, murdered his other child, Abel. Cain was set out and cast away (Genesis 4:1-26), and his descendants committed murder as well. What a start for mankind! It would seem that Satan's sabotage was working. However, God had a plan from the beginning. He created the world, and He created a plan of salvation even before the foundation of the world had been laid. It

was His will that Jesus would eventually become a physical reality and satisfy the sacrificial atonement for sin (and death). But this would be established through the lineage of Seth.

5 God began that sequence of events with the birth of Seth. Seth is the *third* son born to Adam (Eve). The lineage of Seth represents new life from death. Contrasted with the lineage of Cain, the generations of Seth can be traced all the way to Jesus, our Redeemer.

6 Now, the lineage all to Jesus can truly begin. The *sixth* generation from Adam on Cain's side, we find the murderer Lamech, a taker of life. The *sixth* generation from Adam on Seth's side (or the *seventh* generation from God) is Enoch, who never experience physical death (Genesis 5:21-24). According to what is learned from the Bible, that which is holy and righteous does not die. But that which is unholy and unrighteous will be destroyed.

7 Enoch's son, Methuselah, would be the oldest human to ever live. He was *seventh* from Adam ... and his son, Lamech, *seventh* from Seth, (yes, the same name as Cain's murdering descendent), would have a son named Noah.

[Notes 8-10]

This section establishes the general nature of man and God. It describes judgment and destruction and their causes. However, it also includes salvation and a new beginning as purposed by God. It initiates the history leading up to the establishment of the Hebrews (Israel) as a nation and the establishment of other nations that are adversaries of Israel (and God).

8 The lineage of Seth extends to Noah, the *eighth* generation. A new beginning (*tenth* generation from God) illustrates divine order. God did not lose control of His creation by Satan's hand. The story of Noah depicts the nature of God. He is holy and He is in control. Thus, He must cast away or destroy that which is evil. However, it is His desire to save that which is otherwise lost and doomed to destruction.

There will always be those who will be destroyed (because of their unholiness), but there will also be those who can and will be saved (because of God's grace). Noah was not only the *eighth* generation from Seth. There were also *eight* people who were saved to start a new beginning.

9 Noah had *three* sons. They were Shem, Ham, and Japheth. These three sons and subsequent descendants of Noah will represent three characteristics of the nature of God. The descendents of Noah would of course go on and populate the whole world and make the various peoples of the world.

The first line (Japheth) will depict the grace and mercy bestowed by God to those who are unworthy but still loves God. Japheth had *seven* sons. They were, in order, Gomer, Magog, Madai, Javan, Tubal, Meshsch, and Tiras. (Genesis 10:2-5) The *fourth* son was Javan. The descendants of Japheth through Javan will be the Gentiles. A study of Paul and the New Testament will address the fact that after the Jews rejected Christ as Messiah and Savior, the Gentiles accepted Christ as Messiah and Savior.

The next line (Ham) depicts the unrighteousness of man and thus subsequent destruction. Ham had *four* sons. They were Cush, Mizraim, Phut, and Canaan. (The *fourth* was Canaan.) The descendents would produce the people of Assyria and Babylon (Mesopotamians), Philistines and Canaanites, as well as others, who will play a role in the events and accounts of the Bible as adversaries of the Hebrews (Israelites) and are ultimately defeated.

It is the descendants of and the listing of these that are most interesting. The descendants of Cush went on to form the nations of Babylon, Assyria, and Mesopotamia in general. The descendants of Mizraim include Ludim, Anamim, Lehabim, Napthulim, Pathrusim, Caslubim, and Caphtorim. Caslubim is listed *sixth*, and they went on to become the Philistines. Canaan's descendants include Sidon and Heth by name, but Scripture continues by listing further descents differently. These include the Jebusites, Amorites, Girgasites, Hivites, Arkites, Sinites, Avadites, Zemarites, and Hamathites (Genesis 10:6-20). Including the Canaanites, these nations or tribes would number *twelve.* All of these nations were specifically singled out as to be overthrown and defeated by the Israelites as they settled throughout Canaan after the Exodus.

Shem had *five* sons. They were Elam, Asshur, Arphaxad, Lud, and Aram. Remember the number *five* represents grace.

10 The *third* son born to Shem was Arphaxad. It would be through this lineage that Jesus would come. Thus, the line of Shem can be traced all the way to the birth of Christ, the Messiah through Arphaxad. It follows the accounts of Adam and Cain and the great Flood and Noah. It depicts the line from which the Savior (Jesus) would emerge and reclaim the holiness, which man had lost.

[Notes 11-20]

It sets the groundwork for the establishment of the Hebrew nation (Israel) and analogous historic descriptions and accounts that occur as the message of God develops. In addition to Israel, it describes the beginnings and destruction of other nations as purposed by God. As this history develops and is studied,

11 Terah is *ten* generations from Noah. The idea of divine and ordinal perfection can be seen here. It is only after these *ten* generations can the establishment of the Hebrews as purposed by God can begin. Terah had three sons. They were Abram, Nahor and Haran. Of course the lineage of the Hebrews and Jesus would come from Abram. But Nahor and Haran's descendents are important to discuss.

12 Haran had a son named Lot. Unlike Abram, Lot's philosophy was more like "a bird in the hand is better than two in a bush." He saw better pastures in other places. He and Abraham parted ways, and he wound up in the region of Sodom and Gomorrah, synonymous with sin. However, as an act of grace, God allowed Lot and his family to escape the doom and destruction of Sodom and Gomorrah. However, his wife became a pillar of salt and perished. In an unknowing incestuous relationship with his two daughters, he fathered two sons (Genesis 19:15-38). Their descendents would become adversaries of the Israelites.

One of those sons was Moab, whose descendants became the Moabites. During the Exodus, the Moabites would not let the Israelites pass through their territory (Judges 11:17-18), and they later formed an alliance with the Midianites to curse the Israelites (Numbers 22:4). They fought with Israel and Judah but were eventually conquered. Ruth, the great-grandmother of King David, was a Moabitess. The Moabites were forbidden to worship in the temple "to the tenth generation" (Deuteronomy 23:3-5). Through Jesus Christ, however, all peoples of the world have access to God, now.

The other son was Ammon. His descendents were the Ammonites who also vexed the Israelites during the Exodus and after the Exile (Nehemiah 4:1-8).

[13] Nahor had a daughter named Rebecca who would be the wife of Isaac and mother of Jacob, later named Israel. His grand-son, Laban, had two daughters, Leah and Rachel. They would be the wives of Jacob. They and their handmaidens (slaves) Zilpah and Bilhah would be the mothers of the sons of Israel, later known as the tribes of Israel.

[14] Abram later became known as Abraham. Abraham is the twenty-first (*three* x *seven*) generation from God and *tenth* generation from Shem. Scripture records that Abram's family left Ur of Chaldees to live in Canaan. But they came to Haran and dwelt there instead. Genesis 12:1 says, "Now the Lord had said unto Abram, get out of your country and from your kindred, and from your father's house unto a land that I will show you." Terah, Abram's father, had tarried in Haran and had not continued toward Canaan. In addition, God would establish His lineage all the way to Jesus through Abram. Although Abram would stumble along the way, his faith would set an example.

Abraham is considered the father of the Hebrew nation. It is his faith and integrity that is defined in Scripture (Hebrews 11:8-12). God had promised him, no other, that he would father a nation that basically could not be counted (Genesis 12:1-3; 13:14-17). This not only included the story of the Hebrews (Jews) but also all of those who accept Christ as the Messiah and their Savior (Romans 11:25-33),

Hebrew 6:13-20). However, Abraham's wife Sarah could not bear children. Not wanting God's timetable but his own, Abram fathered Ishmael from his wife's slave Hagar. He fathered a son named Ishmael. Although he was Abraham's firstborn, he was not of God's will from which Jesus the Messiah would come.

However, in Abram and his wife's old age, they still conceived (in God's timetable), and Isaac was born. Sarah, Abraham's wife was well beyond child bearing age and that is why she devised the plan for Abraham to father a child by her slave (Hagar). However, it was God's plan for HER to be the mother and not Hagar. God intervened and allowed Sarah to become a mother and gave birth to Isaac. It is through this lineage that Christ came, not that of Ishmael.

[15] In time, Sarah would die, and Abram would remarry. He would marry Keturah. They would have six sons. The *fourth* would be Midian, from which the Midianites came. The wife of Moses was a Midianite.

[16] Isaac was Abraham's only son through Sarah. It was the story of Abraham willing to sacrifice this only son, Isaac, that we understand the sacrifice of faith and the concept of the scapegoat or the replacement sacrifice (Genesis 22:1-13). God would sacrifice His only begotten Son (Jesus). Jesus would essentially replace that sacrifice.

Isaac was *forty* years old when he took Rebekah as his wife (Genesis 25:20). Rebekah is the great-granddaughter (*fourth* generation) of Terah. Remember, it was that family that left Ur of Chaldees. Isaac is the grandson of Terah (the *third* generation). This led to combining of the *third* and *fourth* generation in the oneness of marriage through Rebekah. The resulting offspring would be Jacob (or Israel)! Isaac was sixty years old (*two* x *three* x *ten*) when Esau and Jacob were born (Genesis 25:26).

[17] Scripture is clear that Esau and Jacob fought in their mother's (Rebekah) womb (Genesis 25:22–3). There is always conflict between that which is good and that which is evil. Satan is the long term adversary of God. Esau was willing to forsake family heritage for a seemingly insignificant trade

(Genesis 25:29-34). Such is sin (evil). Man gives away his heritage and his right of creation to pursue that which is seemingly more pleasant, if but only a brief time. God created Adam first. But Adam sinned, and death entered the world. But God would allow another generation to conquer death. It was the oldest (Cain) who killed the youngest. Again, it was the oldest that forsook his rightful place. Thus, God saw fit for the younger (Jacob) to rise above the older.

Like his father, Isaac, Esau was *forty* years old when he took Bashemath, the daughter of Ishmael (Genesis 36:3), as well as others as his wives. The direct descendents of Esau would become the Edomites (Genesis 36:1-9). The descendants of Ishmael and Esau would become the present-day Arabs.

18 The name Jacob means "supplanter." But his name was changed to Israel, meaning "prince." In Genesis 32, Jacob wrestled with an angel and claimed to have seen God "face-to-face and my life is preserved." Jacob's family would go on to become the Israelites and lineage from which Jesus would come. He represents the end of the patriarchs from which God's plan of salvation would come.

Jacob had a first love named Rachel (Genesis 29:18). But he was tricked into marrying her sister, Leah. Jacob had to work for Laban (his uncle) for a total of *fourteen* years (*two x seven*) years in order to marry Rachel.

Legally, however, Leah was Jacob's first wife. The *third* born was Levi, whose descendants would become the priests. The *fourth* son was Judah, from which the human linage to Jesus would pass.

But Jacob would eventually have *twelve* sons, *six* from Leah and *two* from Zilpah, Leah's handmaiden, *two* from Bilhah, Rachel's handmaiden, and *two* from his beloved Rachel. Early on, Rachel was barren; however, Joseph was eventually born. Joseph was Jacob's firstborn of his first love Rachel. God used that to illustrate His nature.

19 Joseph was later sold into slavery by his own brothers. However, it is interesting that the firstborn of Rachel (Joseph) was sold by his own brothers into slavery to the Ishmaelites and that Joseph was taken to Egypt (Genesis 37:28). In Scripture, Egypt has been symbolic of

slavery. The loss of an offspring of a first love is certainly tragic. Jacob (Israel) thought he had lost Joseph, the first born of Rachel. Rachel would later die in childbirth to the youngest of Jacob's sons, Benjamin (Genesis 35:17–19).

However, Joseph would eventually rise to great authority in Egypt, and in a time of a famine, he was able to get the rest of his family down into Egypt for food. Scripture indicates that there were seventy (*seven* x *ten*) in all (Exodus 1:5). But this number grew for the Exodus from Egypt.

[20] Of the twelve tribes of Israel that would obtain an inheritance or land in Canaan following the Exodus from Egypt, the Levites would become the priests and would not inherit a section of land, and Joseph, the son sold into slavery, would not receive an inheritance. It is interesting that the tribe of Joseph would not inherit territory in Canaan. However, that would fall to his sons Ephriam and Manesseh. In fact, Paul would claim in the New Testament that Christians are rightful heirs of God, though not of blood relation, but of adoption (Ephesians 1:4-5, Roman 8:9-16, Romans 9:4-11).

The analogy is that Christians are adopted by God and paid for (redeemed) through Jesus Christ. Jesus paid the redemptive price by dying for our sins (Titus 2:11-15, Galatians 4:1-7). Through this act of redemption, we became heirs of God ... or regained that (fellowship) which was originally lost. Paul explains this in the New Testament, but literal examples to describe this act is given through the awarding of "The Promised Land" to the tribe of Manessa and Ephriam, and later to Ruth, the Moabititess.

[Notes 21-23]

[21] According to Scripture, *three* generations are listed between Levi (*third* son of Israel) and Moses. Earlier pieces of the story illustrate the nature of sin and the required sacrifices to pay for it. This part of the story shows the necessity of the holiness and righteousness of the priests, who on behalf of the people offer the sacrifice (Leviticus 21). The sacrifice for payment for the sin of man is great. Priests, from the

tribe of Levi were to act as a mediator and offer the sacrifices on behalf of the people. However, even the priests that offered had to go through a "cleansing" ritual. Jesus was not only the sacrifice, but the mediator or High Priest as well (Hebrews 5:1-10, 8:6-13). However, man cannot only pay for the sacrifice, but the priests to offer it are unholy as well. The emphasis is placed on the fact that man cannot possibly redeem himself. Only a holy God is able to redeem. The redemption story leading up to Jesus is emphasized here.

[22] Judah was the *fourth* son of Jacob. It interesting that Jesus, the prophet, priest, and king (and Savior) would come from Judah's lineage. Judah was also the *fourth* generation from Abraham. Judah had two sons, Er and Onan. Both "were wicked in the sight of the Lord" (Genesis 38:7–10) Er was married to a woman named Tamar, but God killed him. Onan was to marry Tamar, and he was supposed to raise up his brother's lineage; however, he was too self-centered and would not do it. God killed him as well. Judah promised Tamar to another younger son, Shelah, but she would have to wait until he grew up.

But that promise never came to be. Pretending to be a prostitute, Tamar tricked Judah and conceived twins by their union. During the birth, Zarah was seemingly born first, as his hand came out first, and the midwife put a scarlet thread around his hand. But he drew it back, and Pharez was the true firstborn instead (Genesis 38:24-30). It has been said that there is a scarlet thread that runs through the entire Bible. This scarlet thread (blood) actually belongs to Jesus. There is an actual event that depicts this! Jesus would be born as a descendent of Pharez (Luke 3:33) and not Zarah. As Satan tries to deceive us into what is believed to be life, instead it is not. Some may recognize Satan and the good life he may bring. However, they soon recognize he is not the true one and as Jesus is the truth and the life (John 14:6)

[23] From Judah, there are *seven* generations to Boaz and Ruth. It is the love story of Ruth and Boaz that illustrates the importance of redemption. Boaz was the only true kinsman able to redeem the property of Naomi (Ruth 4:1-10). Ruth was a Moabitess (Ruth 2:2), but she was able to obtain a new life.

[Notes 24-29]

24 David now becomes the primary focal point in the story of the Bible. King David is the great-grandson of Ruth and Boaz or *three* generations later. The framework of God's purpose of Scripture as depicted in the events leading up to King David becomes clearer.

The first mention of the first king of Israel, Saul, occurs in a story about Saul looking for his father's donkey, and he could not even do that (1 Samuel 9). Yet, that is who the children of Israel chose as their king.

The first mention of David occurs in the story about David playing the harp before King Saul in order to soothe him (1 Samuel 16:13-23). Following that is the story of David defeating the giant Goliath and the Philistine army (1 Samuel 17:23-58). Thus, there is a very significant contrast between King Saul and the soon-to-be King David.

David was the youngest of *eight* sons born to Jesse. David ruled for *forty* years as king of Israel, *seven* in Hebron and then *thirty-three* in Jerusalem. (Jesus was thirty-three when He was crucified.) It is also interesting that David is thirty-three generations from Adam.

David had *six* sons born in Hebron. But he had *four* sons born of Bathsheba in Jerusalem.

The *third* son was Nathan, and the *fourth* son was Solomon. From the accounts of Matthew and Luke, the lineage from Solomon and Nathan would lead to Joseph and Mary respectively. Of course Joseph was not the biological father of Jesus, but Mary was the biological mother of Jesus. This genealogical loop begins with David; God's chosen King of Israel, and ends with Jesus, the King of Kings and Lord of Lords.

25 The *third* son of David born in Jerusalem was Nathan. There would be *forty* generations listed between Nathan and Jesus according to the book of Luke. Saul, David, and Solomon would each serve *forty* years as king of Israel. Recall that the number *forty* depicts trial and hardships followed by another period. This line would pass through Mary, and end with Jesus. The birth of Jesus, and His subsequent life, crucifixion and resurrection certainly began a new period in the purpose of God.

[26] The *fourth* son of David born in Jerusalem was Solomon. Counting David and Jesus inclusively, there are twenty-eight generations as listed in the book of Matthew. Unfortunately, following the illustrious time period of Solomon as king, the nation of Israel split into a Northern Kingdom (referred to as Israel) only to be utterly destroyed by Assyria in 721 BC and the Southern Kingdom (referred to as Judah). Judah was not totally destroyed but a remnant was exiled to Babylon.

These include two fourteen generations that are divided by the Babylonian exile. (The gematria of David in the Hebrew language is *fourteen*.) From David to Josiah is *fourteen* generations, and from Jechoniah (where the exile began) to Jesus is *fourteen* generations.

[27] The Southern Kingdom (Judah) was taken into captivity by Babylon in 587 BC. The captivity lasted about seventy years, when the Persians (Medes) overthrew the Babylonians and allowed the Jews to return to their homeland. It was never utterly destroyed.

[28] Although Joseph was not the biological father of Jesus, he is included "because he (Joseph) was of the house and lineage of David" (Luke 2:4). Thus the ancestry of Jesus is complete.

[29] There is a song titled 'Jesus, Jesus' written by Gloria Gaither. The opening words are "Jesus, Jesus, there's just something about that name". How many songs have been written about Jesus? How many sermons and commentaries have mentioned the name of ... Jesus? What other name in human record has the effect on human life and behavior as does the name of Jesus? Notice the culmination of the lineage of Jesus from the kingly side of David through Solomon, which would go through the physical person of Joseph, the husband of Mary, the mother of Jesus. Of course, Jesus was born of a virgin. But it does demonstrate the kingly lineage all the way to Adam ... and to God.

Through Nathan, there are *sixty-six* generations listed from Shem to Jesus (inclusive of Shem and Jesus). Jesus was fully man. Including God and Jesus (as one), there are *seventy-seven* generations listed. It illustrates God's ultimate, complete and fullness of His creation and salvation through Jesus. Is it any wonder that one of the last statements exclaimed by Jesus as hung on the cross before He died was, "It is finished" (John 19:30)? How can there be doubt that the Bible is truly *Fitly Framed Together*?

CHAPTER 5

Chronology of the Bible

The Significance of History Recorded in the Bible

Quite possibly the number-one reason why we believe the Bible is exclusively the Word of God is because of its chronological order. The Bible begins with the book of Genesis, which tells us about the *beginning* of all things and ends with the book of Revelation, which tells us about the *end* of all things.

For example, we read about the following in Genesis:

1. The beginning of creation
2. The beginning of sin
3. The beginning of prophecies
4. The beginning of salvation
5. The beginning of death

Conversely, in the book of Revelation, we read about the following:

1. The beginning of a new creation
2. The end and punishment for sin
3. The fruition of all prophecies
4. The reward of salvation
5. The end of death

God made space and time. In the realm of physics, both space and time are physical. The opportunity of time is important. Once it is gone, it is gone forever. Earth is not like that in the spiritual world, where there is no physical space or time. However, at the present, we do not live in the spiritual worlds. We live in the physical world, where there is time.

We measure time in units of seconds, minutes, hours, days, weeks, months, years, decades, centuries, millennium, and eons. Because time is real and we live within the current time, time is precious. Thus it becomes important to invest in time.

Any historical writing can be regarded as dependent on the limits of human knowledge as it is presented in a text. However, as we can record the time past, we can study it and better understand our physical relationship to this physical world and others who are part of the world. As such, there is an opportunity for involvement and interaction with one another. Sometimes this interaction is good. However, it is unfortunate that in most cases, because of man's sin, pride, and unwillingness to recognize the One who created the physical (as well as spiritual), history has shown this interaction to be bad.

Although the Bible is not intended to be read strictly as a history book, the fabric of the Bible covers all of history, detailing the beginning and outlining the end. The purpose of the Bible is not to explain or support science and archeology. Its purpose, of course, is to explain the nature of God. But in doing so, it does describe events of history that fit within the chronology of man.

The following chronology is certainly not a complete history of all human occurrences. In addition, there are, of course, inherent difficulties in developing a chronology of this type. The dates given are sometimes only approximations. Scholars differ on some exact dates, and some events are uncertain. But it does show a fairly accurate picture of past human events. The stories and writings of the books of the Bible are also shown within the history of human events.

Chronology of Human Events

Time Event

Prehistoric Era

15 billion BC—According to science, "big bang" occurs.
10 billion BC—According to science, solar system develops.
5 billion BC—According to science, earth develops.
1 billion BC—Archeozoic Era
825 million BC—Proterozoic Era
500 million BC—Paleozoic Era
185 million BC—Mesozoic Era
100 million BC—Jurassic Period (age of the dinosaurs)
65 million BC—According to science, dinosaurs become extinct.
3 million BC—Cenozoic Era (Fossil remains of "Lucy" formed.)

1 million BC—
4000 BC—Sumerian/Mesopotamian development (fertile crescent, writing with symbols) Chinese/Indian civilizations
3500 BC—Boats with sails, wheeled wagons, potter's wheel invented.
3200 BC—Phoenicians (written alphabet developed)
3100 BC—Egypt united—Old Kingdom

3000 BC—Copper/bronze, metal works, man plows with animals
2700 BC—Egyptian pharaohs, pyramids built.

2169 BC—Abram (Abraham) is born.
2069 BC—Isaac is born.
2100 BC—Egypt—Middle Kingdom (Twelfth Dynasty)
2069 BC—Isaac is born.
2009 BC—Jacob (Israel) is born.

2000 BC—Chaldean/Mesopotamian (Semitic Amorites)

1900 BC—Abraham receives a message from God, leaves Ur of the Chaldees, initiating Hebrew beginnings.
1879 BC—Jacob (Israel) and family go down into Egypt.

1800 BC—Egypt—Second Intermediate Period (Hyksos)
1760 BC—Hammurabi's Code is written. (Babylon origin))

1700 BC—Stonehenge is built in Great Britain.

1600 BC
1570 BC—Egypt—New Kingdom (Eighteenth Dynasty)
—Thutmose III (Egypt)
—Queen Hatshepsut (Egypt)
1529 BC—Moses is born.

1500 BC—Amenhotep II (Egypt) and China (Shang Dynasty)
1449 BC—The Hebrew Exodus from Egypt occurs. Its influence on religion and life of Israel is beyond imagination. Concepts of physical rule for an orderly life emerge. Concepts of bondage to sin (Egypt) and the power of God to conquer take shape.

> Moses writes **Genesis**, ***Exodus, Leviticus, Numbers, Deuteronomy***. *Genesis means the beginning and is a book of origins. Leviticus, Numbers were written as instructional sources of procedures for living. Deuteronomy is quoted more than eighty times in the New Testament.*

1409 BC—The Hebrews finally enter the Promised Land.
—Story of Joshua, Rahab the harlot, and fall of Jerico.

1400 BC

__Joshua__ is written. It continues the history of Israel as begun in the Pentateuch. God wishes to provide for His Creation ... and His people.

Israel becomes a kingdom ruled by judges.
1369 BC—Pharaoh Amenhotep IV (Egypt)
1330 BC—Pharaoh Tutankhamen (Egypt)

__Judges__ is written. It tells how God raises the weak to confound the strong.

1300 BC
1290 BC—Pharaoh Ramses II (Egypt)
1250 BC—Queen Nefertiti (Egypt)

1200 BC—Stories of Gideon, Samson occur.
1100 BC

The story of __Ruth__ occurs here. It is an incomparable love story. She marries Boaz, becoming an ancestor to Jesus. It symbolizes redemption.

The stories of __Samuel 1 and 2, Kings 1 and 2__, as well as __Chronicles 1 and 2__ occur here. These books describe issues and actions in the lives of men and nations as examples of what God is saying. God rules in the lives of men and nations as well as judgments and blessings.

1053 BC—King Saul (Israel)
1013 BC—King David (Israel)

1000 BC
973 BC—King Solomon (Israel)
969 BC—Temple construction is begun.
962 BC—Temple construction is complete.

> ***Psalms*** *is written. It tells of utterances of the heart, wisdom, love, hopelessness; a living testimony. Human emotions, such as praise, adoration, thanksgiving, fear, despair.*
>
> ***Proverbs*** *is written. It tells of wisdom and of moral quality. It compares the true wisdom of God to the wisdom of man.*
>
> ***Ecclesiastes*** *is written. It tells that life apart from God is vanity. All earthly goals when pursued as an end in themselves is vanity and leads to emptiness.*
>
> ***Song of Solomon*** *is written. It extols human love and God's love.*
>
> *The story of* ***Job*** *occurs. It tells of unreserved consecration to the Lord.*

950 BC
933 BC—Israel's Kingdom splits—Judah (*Rehoboam* is king) and Israel (*Jeroboam is king*)
915 BC—Judah—*Abijah (Abijam)*
912 BC—Judah—*Asa*
911 BC—Israel—*Nadab*
910 BC—Israel—*Basha*

900 BC—Rise of Assyria (Nineveh is capital)
887 BC—Israel—*Elah*
886 BC—*Israel—Zimri*
—Israel—*Omri*
875 BC—Israel—*Ahaz*
—Story of *Ahab*/Jezebel/Elijah
874 BC—Judah—*Jehoshaphat*
855 BC—Israel—*Ahaziah*
854 BC—Israel—*Joram*
850 BC—Judah—*Jehoram (Joram)*

—Story of Elisha
843 BC—Israel- *Jehu*
—Judah—*Ahaziah (Jehoahaz)*
—Judah—*Athaliah*
—Judah—*Joash (Jehoash)*
820 BC—Israel—*Jehohaz*
806 BC—Israel—*Joash*
803 BC—Judah—Amaziah

800 BC— ***Joel** is written. It tells of a vision of the gospel age, ingathering of the nations.*
790 BC—Israel—*Jeroboam II*
787 BC—Judah—*Uzziah*
760 BC— *Story of **Jonah** occurs. It tells how Jonah goes to Nineveh and preaches God's salvation. The people respond and actually turn to God. It shows that God is interested in all people (not just the Hebrews).*

Hosea *is written. It tells of God's amazing love and that He will one day will be the God of all nations.*

753 BC—City of Rome is founded.
750 BC ***Amos** is written. It illustrates that God's house will yet rule.*
749 BC—Judah—*Jotham*
748 BC—Israel—*Zechariah*
—Israel—*Shallum*
—Israel—*Menahem*
—Israel—*Pekah*
745 BC ***Isaiah** is written. It illustrates that God has remnant, and for it, a Glorious future. Judah would be the messianic nation to the world.*

***Micah** is written. It illustrates the universal reign of the Prince of Bethlehem, Jesus.*

741 BC—Judah—*Ahaz*
738 BC—Israel—*Pekahiah*

730 BC—Israel—*Hoshea* (last king of Israel)
726 BC—Judah—*Hezekiah*

721 BC—Fall of the Northern Kingdom (Israel) to Assyria

700 BC
697 BC—Judah—*Manasseh*
641 BC—Judah—*Amon*
639 BC—Judah- *Josiah*
—Reformations of Judah take place under young King *Josiah*
630 BC ***Nahum*** *is written. He preaches doom to Nineveh the capital of Assyria.*
626 BC— ***Jeremiah*** *is written. He preaches Jerusalem's sin and doom.*
Zephaniah *is written. It illustrates the coming of a New Revelation.*
612 BC—Nineveh (Assyria) is destroyed by the Medes.
610 BC ***Habakkuk*** *is written. It illustrates the ultimate triumph for Jehovah's people.]*

608 BC—Nebuchadnezzar, King of Babylon, begins the overthrow of Judah and begins to exile many of the Jews.
—Daniel is taken and exiled to Babylon.
—King *Josiah* is killed by Pharaoh.
—King Jehoahaz is carried to Egypt.
—Judah (*Jehoikim* becomes King of Judah)
606 BC—Fall of Assyria (Nineveh) to Babylon and Rise of Babylon
—Nebuchadnezzar King of Babylon defeats Egypt (Assyria) at Carchemish.

600 BC—Judah (*Jehoichin*)
597 BC—Exile of Judah continues. Ten thousand carried into captivity, including Ezekiel and King Jehoichin.
—Judah—*Zedekiah* (Last King of Judah)

Ezekiel *is written. It tells of the fall of Jerusalem, restoration and glorious future. Though there is judgment, there is victory.*

***Daniel** is written. It is a book of prophesy.*

—Story of Shadrach, Meshach, Abednego and fiery furnace (King Nebuchadnezzar of Babylon) occurs.

587 BC—Fall of Southern Kingdom (Judah) to King Nebuchadnezzar of Babylon is completed.

***Lamentations** is written. It laments the fall of Judah.*
***Obadiah** is written. It predicts the fall of Edom.*

563 BC—Gautama Buddha is born (initiating Buddhism).
551 BC—Confucius is born (initiating Confucianism).
—Story of "fingers on the wall" (King Belshazzar of Babylon)

538 BC—Fall of Babylon and Rise of Persia
—Cyrus, King of Medo-Persian Empire decreed that Israel could return from exile and build the temple again.
520 BC—Story of Daniel and the lion's den (King Darius I of Persia).
***Haggai** is written. It describes the rebuilding of the temple, but tells of the coming of a greater temple.*
Zechariah *is written. It illustrates the coming of the King (Jesus), His house and kingdom, and the rebuilding of another temple.*
516 BC—The rebuilding of the temple in Jerusalem takes place.

500 BC
490 BC—Battle of Marathon (Near Athens; Greece against Darius I of Persia)
478 BC— *Story of **Esther** occurs here. She marries Xerxes (Ahasuerus) King of Persia.*
—Story of Haman/Mordecai and the Feast of Purim is instituted.
470 BC—Socrates (Greece) is born.
460 BC—Democritus (Greece) is born.
457 BC— ***Ezra** is written. It calls the people together in solemn assembly for the renewal of the covenant.*

450 BC—Twelve Tables for Roman law

444 BC— ***Nehemiah** is written. It describes the rebuilding of the walls of Jerusalem.*

430 BC— ***Malachi** is written. As the last book of the Old Testament it is the closing message of a Messianic nation.*

427 BC—Fall of Persia and Rise of Greece

—Plato (Greece) is born

400 BC

384 BC—Aristotle (Greece) is born

331 BC—Alexander the Great (of Greece) defeats Darius III of Persia.

320 BC—Ptolemy I, a general of Alexander the Great, captures Jerusalem.

—Expansion of the Seleucid Empire following the partitioning of Alexander the Great's empire.

300 BC

220 BC—Great Wall of China is completed.

217 BC—Saturnalia—winter solstice/worship by Romans originates (at later date to celebrate Christmas on December 25).

200 BC

167 BC—Judas "the Maccabee" leads a revolt against the Seleucid Empire.

165 BC—Hanukkah, or the "Festival of Lights" was instituted in Jerusalem, commemorating the restoration of Jewish worship in the temple.

130 BC—Origins of the Pharisees and Sadducees occur during these times.

146 BC—Roman Empire begins (with conquest of Carthaginians and Corinthians)

—Fall of Greece

100 BC

63 BC—Pompey invades Palestine. Roman rule begins there.

46 BC—Julian calendar is created.

44 BC—Julius Caesar is assassinated.

—Octavian (Caesar Augustus) becomes Emperor of Rome.

37 BC—Herod the Great (son of Antipater) rules as King of Judea and is subject to Rome.

30 BC—Mark Anthony and Cleopatra die.

20 BC—Herod begins the rebuilding/remodeling of the temple in Jerusalem.

4 BC—Birth of Jesus Christ (initiating Christianity)

Events of Matthew, Mark, Luke, John *(Gospels of Christ) occur.*

—Tiberius becomes Emperor of Rome.

30 AD—Crucifixion and resurrection of Jesus occur.

32 AD—Conversion of Saul takes place.

Events of **Acts** *occur. It tells of stories of rejection of Christ by Jews and acceptance by Gentiles and treatment and acceptance of the early church.*

—Caligula becomes Emperor of Rome.

50 AD—Paul's first missionary journey begins.

51 AD—Claudius becomes Emperor of Rome.

55 AD—Paul's second missionary journey begins.

1 Corinthians as well as 1 and 2 Thessalonians *are written. These are letters of instruction and a glimpse of the early church and events leading up the second coming of Christ.*

60 AD—Paul's third missionary journey begins.

Romans, 2 Corinthians *are written. It describes the basic Christian philosophy and how to handle church issues.*

Galatians, James *are written. It describes faith and works, and the breadth of the Biblical message.*

Colossians, Philemon, Philippians *are written. These are considered the prison epistles (of Paul) and describe the redemptive relationship of man to God.*

Ephesians, 1 and 2 Timothy *are written. These letters from Paul are an* exhortation and a charge to the faithful.

***Titus** is written. It describes the connection between faithful men, godliness and good works.*
***Hebrews** is written. It illustrates that only Christ can guarantee to a believer entrance to heaven.*

64 AD—During the reign of Emperor Nero, Rome burns.
***1 and 2 Peter** are written. It illustrates that all have access to God's grace and mercy and Christ will return.*

65 AD—Paul is martyred in Rome.

70 AD—Jerusalem (and temple) is destroyed by the Romans.
***Jude** is written. It warns against Gnosticism.*

81 AD—Domitian becomes Emperor of Rome.
90 AD ***1, 2, 3 John, The Revelation** are written. They tell of fellowship with God compared to heresy. Revelation also tells of the final judgment of God and end of time and space.*

100 AD
150 AD—Claudius Galen is a Roman physician to the Gladiators.
154 AD—Anicetus (Bishop of Rome) proclaims himself Pope, initiating a universal Christian religion called the Roman Catholic Church.

200 AD

300 AD
306 AD—Emperor Constantine establishes "new Rome" at Constantinople. Division of the Roman Catholic Church, development of the Greek Orthodox Church and the Russian Orthodox Church.

389 AD—St. Patrick is born in England.

395 AD—The Roman Empire is divided into the Eastern Empire and Western Empire.

400 AD
410 AD—Rome is sacked by the Visigoths.
450 AD—Events of Attila the Hun begins.
455 AD—Rome sacked by the Vandals.

476 AD—Fall of Rome (to German forces)

500 AD—**Middle Ages**

523 AD—Gregorian calendar is created.

570 AD—Muhammad is born.

600 AD

621 AD—Muhammad receives heavenly messages, revered as a prophet, writing of the Koran, initiating Islam.
690 AD—Dome of the Rock, Al-Aqsa mosque built in place where the temple once stood in Jerusalem.

700 AD
750 AD—St. Boniface (of England) uses fir trees to explain the Trinity to people in France.
762 AD—Baghdad is built as capital of Islamic Abbasids to rid infidels (built with stones from ancient Babylon).
795 AD—Holy Roman Empire begins (Charlemagne and Pope Leo III).

800—900 AD—Vikings pillage England, venture to North America?

Medieval Ages
1000 AD—Feudalism in Europe (population of world equals 275 million)

1065 AD—Visitors from Europe begin to visit the Holy Land. Crusades begin, clashing with warring Islam.

1100 AD
1162 AD—Genghis Kahn (Mongolia) is born.
1187 AD—Muslims take Jerusalem.

1200 AD—French author Cretien DeTraye writes (but does not complete) story, including the Holy Grail.
1215 AD—The Magna Carta is written.
1235 AD—Notre Dame Cathedral is built.

1291 AD—Last of the Crusades occur.

1300 AD–1600 AD—The **Renaissance** (New Birth) begins.

1400 AD

1452 AD—Leonardo da Vinci is born
1453 AD—Fall of Constantinople (to Islam).
1454 AD—Gutenberg's printing press (prints the Latin Vulgate Bible).
1475 A.D—Michelangelo is born.
1492 AD—Columbus sails to the New World.

1500 AD
1503 AD—Negro slaves are brought to the Americas.
1517 AD—Martin Luther begins the Protestant Reformation.

1520 AD—Ignatius Loyola initiates Catholic Reformation. Jesuits (against heresy) begin.
1533 AD—John Calvin leads a group to Switzerland (Calvinist).
1534 AD—Henry VIII severs ties with Rome, begin Anglican Church because Pope would not annul his marriage with Catherine in order for him to marry Anne Boleyn.
1545 AD—Council of Trent (to review Catholic dogma, faith plus works, use of Latin, veneration of saints, indulgences, church monarchy ruled by Pope.)

1572 AD—Ten thousand French Huguenots killed in St. Bartholomew massacre.

1574 AD—Spanish Inquisitions occur to rid heresy.

1587 AD—Mary Stuart (Catholic Queen of Scots) beheaded by her cousin Elizabeth (Protestant Queen of England).

1600 AD
1607 AD—Jamestown is established (John Smith, Pocahontas).
1608 AD—First Baptists meet in Amsterdam.

1611 AD—The King James (I) Bible is first printed.

1616 AD—Galileo and Copernicus are convicted of heresy by the Roman Catholic Church. They claimed that Earth as well as the other planets actually went around the Sun. The Sun was the center of an organized arrangement called the solar system.
1620 AD—Pilgrims land at Plymouth Rock.

1667 AD—*Paradise Lost* is written by John Milton.

1700 AD
1776 AD—United States of America declares its independence from England.

1781 AD—General Cornwallis (England) surrenders to General George Washington (United States).

1800 AD
1803 AD—Louisiana Purchase takes place.
—Rise of the United States of America
1806 AD—Lewis and Clark Expedition occurs.
1822 AD—Joseph Smith started receiving heavenly messages, revered as a prophet, initiating the Mormon Church.
1823 AD—Calvinist Methodists begin.

1848 AD—Texas and California are ceded to the United States by Mexico.

1900 AD—**Modern Times**

1914 AD—World War I begins

1917 AD—Bolshevik Revolution occurs in Russia.
—Rise of the Soviet Union

1918 AD—Paris Peace Conference takes place.

1922 AD—Treaty of 1922 established the Union of Soviet Socialist Republic (USSR).

1934 AD—Hitler becomes chancellor and president (Fuhrer)

1935 AD—Social Security Act passed.

1936 AD—First computer invented.

1941 AD—Japan attacks Pearl Harbor and the United States enters World War II.

1947 AD—Israel becomes a recognized nation.

1957 AD—Space age begins.

1969 AD—Apollo 11, US astronaut Neil Armstrong is the first man to walk on the moon.

1972 AD—Apollo 17 was the last manned flight to the moon by the United States.

1973 AD—Supreme Court case *Roe v. Wade* ruling establishes abortion as legal in the United States.

1975 AD—First personal computer made.

1978 AD—Fifteen American Hostages are taken at US embassy in Iran.

1981 AD—Space shuttle Columbia marks the first of shuttle flights by the United States.

1985 AD—Microsoft Windows is created for the personal computer.

1991 AD—USSR falls

2000 AD. Y2K scare occurs that predicted that all computer-driven services would fail because of the change to a new millennium.

2001 AD—Twin Towers Trade Center in New York are destroyed by Islamic extremists and terrorists.

2003 AD—Space shuttle *Columbia* disintegrates on reentry into the earth's atmosphere on its twenty-seventh mission. Saddam Hussein is deposed from Iraq.

2004 AD—Public display of the Ten Commandments ruled illegal (under separation of church and state).

Christmas displays by municipalities depicting the first Christmas ruled illegal (separation of church and state).

The phrase "Merry Christmas" considered not appropriate. The phrase "Happy Holidays" is considered more politically correct, so as to not offend those of other faiths, such as those who celebrate Hanukkah or Kwanza or other people who do not celebrate the season at all.

2006 AD—Saddam Hussein, former dictator of Iraq, is executed.

2007 AD—Flag ceremonies (twelve steps of folding the American flag) limited as deemed "offensive" to non-Christians.

Televised "Pledge of Allegiance" omits "under God."

"In God We Trust" accidentally omitted on newly coined dollar coins.

Churches are identified as businesses. Therefore, non-tax-exempt status should be revoked.

2010 AD

2011 AD—Osama Bin Laden, instigator of the 9/11 World Trade Towers terrorist act, is killed by US Armed Forces.

2013 AD—Twenty percent of the states in America have by this date sanctioned same-sex marriage. Twenty states have legalized the medical use of marijuana or have legalized its use altogether. Boy Scouts of America consider allowing homosexual men to lead young boys of America.

2015 AD

???? AD—Fall of the United States of America occurs?

???? AD—The second coming of Christ takes place?

???? AD—End of time occurs?

As one looks at the events of history, the effects that the Bible has had on history cannot be taken lightly. The influence that the Bible has had on the records and chronicles of mankind is enormous. To be sure, much misinterpretation has occurred, but its influence is unquestionable. There are no other writings that have influenced the history of man more than the Bible. Of course one would think that any Word of God would have such power of such sway.

EPILOGUE

The American people are subject to the federal tax codes. People might say that the text of this tax code is so enormous and complex that it is ten times thicker than the Bible, and in the past ten years, there have been more than five thousand editions and changes. The Bible, on the other hand, is not that complex and has never changed. What has been written in the Bible and applied to the human race stands alone, firm and unchanging. And although it may seem complex, its message is clear. There is a God. There is sin, and there is a consequence for sin. But God has developed a redemptive plan of salvation to keep us from those consequences. In addition, the Bible teaches ways and means for man to love Him (vertically) and love his fellow man (horizontally) and thus have a better relationship with both God and man.

"So shall my word be that goes forth out of my mouth: it shall not return void, but it shall accomplish that which please, and it shall prosper where I send it" (Isaiah 55:11). "For the word of God is living, and powerful, and sharper than any to edged sword, piercing even to the dividing asunder of soul and spirit, and of the joints of the marrow, and is a discerner of thoughts and intents of the heart" (Hebrews 4:12). As smart and accomplished as one may think mankind is, man could not have literally written the Bible.

There is a continuity and oneness of the message and presentation of the Bible across the Old and New Testaments and is evidence that the Bible is indeed characteristically unique. Christians may live in a bad news world, but they have a good news gospel to tell. Yet too often, Christians are like tea bags that just sit around with little usefulness until they get placed into some hot water. And the non-Christians have so little knowledge of the gospel that they cannot enjoy the happiness and contentment of this physical life, and of course, they will not experience the eternal life in heaven with the One who created it all.

Satan, too, knows Scripture, and because of this, he was able to trick and deceive Jewish leadership. He got them caught up in the statutes, laws, rituals, pomp, and circumstance of worship. And when Jesus, the true Messiah, did come, they could not even recognize him. Christianity is not a religion. It is not of just believing (or faith), but of *behaving.* To be sure, the Bible does speak of God, but from Genesis to the book of Revelation, it speaks of love, grace, mercy, and the redemptive, saving power of Jesus. However, it also speaks of death, destruction, hopelessness, and despair.

The book of Hosea is located about in the middle of the Bible. It classically explains the entire Bible. "O Israel, return to the Lord your God; for you have fallen by your own iniquity ... Who is wise, and he shall understand these things? prudent, and he shall know them? For the ways of the Lord are right, and the just shall walk in them: but the transgressor shall; fall therein" (Hosea 14:1, 9).

Prior to the days of Christopher Columbus, if one thought of the geometric shape of the earth, it was not considered round. In fact, many sailors believed the earth was flat! But in the Bible, we read, "It is he that sits upon the *circle* of the earth: (Isaiah 40:22). We also find, "When he prepared the heavens, I was there: when he drew a *compass (circle)* on the face of the deep" (Proverbs 8:27). It is interesting that hundreds of years before consideration was given to the shape of the earth, God had already spoken about its nature.

The Bible has been designed and written to present the nature of God which includes His love and His hate. He loves His creation but hates sin. This nature of the Scripture is the basis of its purpose.

Because man fell as the result of sin, God's redemptive plan can bring man back to Him. Jesus Himself said, "As my Father has loved me, so have I loved you... These things I have spoken unto you that your joy might remain in you, and that your joy might be full... love one another, as I have loved you." (John 15: 9-12) "Love works no ill to his neighbor...now it is high time to awake out of sleep: for now is our salvation nearer than when we believed. The night is far spent, the day is at hand..." (Romans 13:10-12).

The Bible exhibits unity of thought and purpose by at least forty different human writers over a 1,500 year period. Yet, the principles, doctrines and objectives of Scripture remain the same from the beginning words of the Bible through the end of the Bible. It has survived throughout history attacks and assaults on its content, integrity and purpose. It has influenced human behavior like nothing else. Indeed the Bible has had a remarkable effect on the events of human history and has been the foundation of inspiration to others to write great works of literature and music. It is unlike any other text. Therefore, it must be considered that the Bible comes from God, and that is has a specific meaning and purpose.

The content of this text is not intended to be an exhaustive search and explanation of the topics mentioned concerning the Bible. It is however, intended to show that the writings of the Old Testament and New Testament testify of the oneness and unity of the Bible. It should be enough to spur on future study by those who desire to dig deeper into God's Word. "Man shall not live by bread alone, but by every word that proceeds out of the mouth of God" (Deuteronomy 8:3 and repeated in Matthew 4:4 by Jesus). The Bible is truly *Fitly Framed Together.* Amen.